Stephen Holbrook

The Light In The Darkness

The Official Biography
by James Christie

D0068175

Mage Publishing
Wizards Eight, Sun Inn Cottages, Colton Tadcaster LS24 8EP

First published in Great Britain by Mage Publishing 2000
This second edition also by Mage Publishing 2001
Copyright © James Christie & Stephen Holbrook

ISBN 0-9527109-1-9

"The Light In The Darkness" can be ordered through most major bookshops by quoting the above ISBN code or alternatively by mail order direct from the publishers at the recommended retail price of £6.99 (plus p&p). For details of future publications and to find out where Stephen is demonstrating next, please visit our website at

www.steve-holbrook.co.uk

Printed by TJ International Ltd., Padstow, Cornwall

This book is dedicated to the following people, with love, thanks and gratitude....

For Stephen

Caroline Holbrook, Una Pearce, Roger and Gill Prior.

For James

Joanna, Pat & Don Fairhurst, and the memory of Ossie Rae.

"There are different kinds of spiritual gifts but the same Spirit gives them. There are different ways of serving but the same Lord is served. There are different abilities to perform service but the same God gives ability to everyone for their particular service. The Spirit's presence is shown in some way in each person for the good of all. The Spirit gives one person a message full of wisdom while to another person the same Spirit gives a message full of knowledge. One and the same Spirit gives faith to one person while to another person he gives the power to heal. The Spirit gives one person the power to work miracles; to another the gift of speaking God's message; and yet to another the ability to tell the difference between the gifts that come from Spirit and those which do not. To one person he gives the ability to speak in strange tongues and to another he gives the ability to explain what is said. But it is one and the same Spirit who does all this; as he wishes, he gives a different gift to each person."

St. Paul – from his first letter to The Corinthians

Who has blown out our most precious lantern?
What are these shadows which cloud our sad eyes?
Where is the life that brought us such bounty?
What are these shouts and from where come these cries?

Who is the stranger, this soul of the spirit,
Who carries the star in the palm of his hand?
Why, this is the one who brings light in the darkness
And bids the sun rise on a new Summer land.

Chapter One: The Onion

I first met Stephen Holbrook in the spring of 1999. Our rendezvous was at The Queens Hotel in Leeds and not unusually for a pair of Taureans we were both ten minutes early for the appointment. Although we'd never met before, I had no difficulty in recognising him: *"Well dressed refugee from the hippy 60's"* was one description I'd been given, while *"sexy young Viking"* was another!

As we walked into The Palm Court Lounge and found a vacant table, I had chance to study my companion, and I had to admit that he *did* look more like a Hollywood super star resting between roles than a clairaudient medium with the reputation of being "the most consistently accurate medium working in Britain today."

This plaudit had come from my friend Harry Andrews who is himself a professional clairvoyant of many years' standing. When my company had first become interested in promoting Stephen I'd asked Harry about him, and Harry, on one of his rare trips into the UK from the USA where he now lives and works, had as usual, been loquaciously forthcoming.

'Ah, thinking of doing something with young Holbrook, are you?' he'd beamed over the double gin and tonic I'd bought him in The Old Vic as a prelude to pumping him for some much needed background information.

'Maybe,' I'd answered cautiously. 'Depends rather on what you might be able to tell me.'

'Rock concerts not going too well, then?'

'Nope!' I'd grinned, thinking of the previous month's fiasco in Loughborough.

'Folk festivals falling a bit flat?'

'Yep!' my grin had broadened ruefully when I thought of the fifty-two people who'd turned up to see The National Folk Legend I'd recently booked into the Newark Palace Theatre. Their combined entrance fees had barely covered The Star's hotel bill!

'What about the classical stuff?'

'Works all right in the right venue, but there aren't enough venues.'

'So,' Harry had polished off his drink, 'thinking of going back to your roots and having a crack at promoting a clairvoyant?'

'Like I said before, it depends. If I could find the right person to promote, I think it might be worth considering.'

'Well, you could do worse than use Holbrook – if he's interested.' Harry had eyed me shrewdly, playing with the twiddly bit of his handle bar moustache. 'You've got to bear in mind that he has his own reasonably well established circuit in central Yorkshire, so you might need to dangle a carrot, and if I were Stephen, the carrot that might interest me would be to be promoted out of the county. Work with him on a national level and you might be onto a winner.'

'What's he like?' I'd asked. 'I mean, I know he's got quite a good reputation, but I've never actually seen him work.'

'Oh he's good,' Harry had said promptly. And then, more thoughtfully, leaning back against the old pew bench... 'In fact, he's very *very* good.'

'How good is "very *very* good"?' I'd pushed him. 'As good as Doris Stokes, for example?'

'Oh yes, certainly as good as dear old Doris, and in some ways even better...' he'd fallen silent for a few seconds, paying quiet homage to the woman who'd done so much to bring mediumship to the public eye during the seventies and eighties. 'The thing you need to remember,' he'd continued, 'is that Holbrook is still only in his thirties – half Doris's age when she was at the height of her powers. Providing he looks after himself and nurtures his gift, by the time he's in his fifties and sixties, he'll be formidable!'

'So what is he *like*?' I'd pushed again.

'As a person? Sorry, old love, I don't have the slightest idea, but as a medium? Well, what can I tell you? He's very

6

accurate, very specific, and I suppose from a promoter's point of view, he's all the rest you need him to be. A nice looking fellow – young, fresh, quite dynamic. I've seen a number of his demonstrations and the quality of his evidence is good and he certainly knows how to hold an audience...'

We'd talked for a while after that, and on the strength of what Harry had told me, I'd 'phoned Stephen the following day and we'd set up the meeting at The Queens for the following week. That week had passed, and now here we were, chatting like old friends, and discussing ways in which my company could help enhance Stephen's national profile.

If the truth be told, I was much more concerned to discover just how much Stephen could help me and my ailing little promotions company. But I didn't tell him that. Not then, anyway.

As I say, I'd never met Stephen before that day, and yet... and yet... There was a curious familiarity about him, as though I had not only met him at some time in the past, but had actually known him well.

We talked for over an hour covering a host of various subjects and ideas. For my part this conversation was interspersed with weird flashes of Déjà Vu. As we talked, I watched him and studied him hard.

Promoting shows and concerts was an important string to my bow, but it was by no means the only string. In my "other" work I'd come to learn a lot about people, and although I was not a medium or clairvoyant, I was pretty good at reading people – tuning in to their psychic vibrations and observing the finer nuances of their body language.

I remember that Stephen was excited about some of the ideas that I put to him, and his enthusiastic response and engaging personality encouraged me to open up and give more away of myself than I would normally have done in such circumstances. And yet, of himself, Stephen gave away very little.

7

Oh certainly, he talked of his experiences, and made more than passing reference to some of his close friends and family – he told me what he'd done and where and how he'd done it but he didn't tell me how he *felt* – and I came away from that first meeting knowing that despite his public image of bonhomie and confidence, I would be dealing with a very private man who whilst very emotional, kept those emotions on an iron leash and well out of the public eye. This in itself was quite unusual for most of the mediums and clairvoyants I've ever met are emotional wrecks who are not only quite prepared to wave their neuroses beneath the glare of the public spotlight, but actually seem compelled to do so. It was obvious from the beginning that Stephen was not one of these dubious stereotypes.

Harry had been quite right (as had others) in their physical descriptions of Stephen Holbrook, but they had not prepared me for the zest and almost childlike naiveté of the man's character. To say that he bubbled with fun and excitement is not an over statement – and yet being one of those people who firmly believes that the eyes are the windows to the soul, I was ever mindful of his eyes!

Stephen's eyes, a bright and penetrating shade of blue, could be filled with sparkling laughter one moment and be clouded with sympathy and concern the next. They could be merry with joy, but there were just an odd couple of occasions when his guard slipped a fraction and I caught a fleeting glimpse of flinty steel. I was reminded that no matter how hearty hail fellow well met his surface personality might be, beneath the surface there was a careful man, a business man, and a man who knew himself far better than most.

My Grandmother, a fey old Gypsy lady and a great teacher in my younger years, once likened human beings to eggs and plums. The eggs, she said, were all hard and tough on the outside, but soft and mushy on the inside. The plums, on the other hand, were soft and squidgy on the outside, but hard as stone on the inside. Following this philosophy through to its natural conclusion, Stephen, I decided, was neither egg nor plum, but something of an onion.

You would get to know him, peel off one layer of skin only to be confronted by another – get to know him better, peel off yet another layer of skin, and hey look, there's *still* another to have a go at! Spend some time with him, get to know him really *really* well, peel off half a dozen layers all at once – and damn it all, there would still be more layers to tackle and you'd still be no closer to discovering the essence of the man than you were when you started!

That day, as I left the Queens Hotel to drive back to York, one part of me felt well pleased. I'd done what I considered to be a good deal with Stephen: we'd thrashed out an acceptable arrangement to both of us and on the strength of it I would be promoting him in Ilkley the following month; however, another part of me felt curiously frustrated.

My own levels of psychic perception had been suppressed by Stephen's far more powerful aura, which was something that had not happened to me for a *very* long time. I found that I was fascinated by the multi-faceted enigma of the man, and my curiosity was aroused.

Unless my imagination was playing tricks, it was reasonably clear that we did have some sort of an empathy – I was confident that we could work together and develop a mutually satisfying business relationship, and even on that first day it seemed to me that not only had I found a new business associate, I'd also found a new friend. Indeed, although not clairvoyant in the same sense that Stephen is clairvoyant, my own innate psychic awareness made me feel that there was a purpose to our meeting that neither of us fully understood at the time. Stephen later told me that he had thought pretty much the same thing, although he, like I, had no idea where this new found energy might take us.

I resolved there and then that should our business partnership evolve and progress, I would make a quiet study of this most unusual man, peeling away each layer of the onion until I got to the core of what he was.

As I cruised back along the A64 I explored my motivation in considering such a project and even then the answers were fairly obvious. It wasn't so much a case of *what* he was – it was more a case of the how and the who, and even more importantly, the *why*.

Chapter Two: On Ilkley Moor...

Stephen's first night for Shoestring Promotions was at The King's Hall in Ilkley. It was a cool early summer evening in May – the rest of the country was enjoying a heatwave but in Ilkley an icy wind blew off the crag of Ben Rhyddig and the moors beyond. It was a lazy wind too – it didn't blow around you but cut straight through, and as the hundred or so people bustled into the faded splendour of the old council building, I was glad I'd had the foresight to tell the caretaker to turn the heating full on. Being cold makes me feel unhappy, jittery and on edge, and counting the heads as they pass through the turnstile is always a tense half hour for a promoter at the best of times.

Cold winds apart, there were other more practical reasons for having one or two misgivings, for on the bloody battleground of show business I'd always made it a firm policy not to book an act without first seeing it perform. Okay, so Stephen wasn't exactly what you'd call an "act" but I'd still blown a good few hundred quid promoting someone on their reputation alone. Harry had spoken glowingly of Stephen's capabilities, as indeed had a handful of other people who's opinions I'd sought, and although the psychic sensitive part of my soul told me to relax, the business side of my brain still fretted.

Normally I would have introduced any act that I was promoting, but Stephen said he'd prefer to go on cold. Therefore once the last person had taken their seat there was little I could do other than to slink up to the electrician's control booth at the back of the balcony and give the go-code for the performance to begin. The house lights went down, the stage lights came up, and Stephen Holbrook made his entrance, almost bouncing onto the stage with energy and enthusiasm.

In those first few seconds I began to unwind. Not only did he look good – friendly smile, dancing locks of Nordic fair hair – he also sounded great! I'd talked to him earlier about using a microphone, but he had assured me that his voice would carry and that a mike would only cramp his style. I'd been a bit dubious, but on this first show, hadn't felt like making an issue of it.

I needn't have worried, for his voice, although essentially quite light in timbre, had an unusual resonance and more than sufficient carrying power to fill the large auditorium, and although from his point of view this had to be quite an important demonstration, he showed absolutely no signs of the nervousness that might have been expected.

In Stephen's eyes this was something of an audition night for a promoter who had a line into a chain of small theatres and better venues than the established circuit of provincial town halls that had been his staple diet over the past few years. I don't think he realised at that time that Shoestring really did mean on a *shoestring* – and as I counted the heads in the cavernous King's Hall for the third time, I realised to my dismay that although I'd covered the cost of hiring the theatre and the even greater cost of the advertising, I was a long way short of being able to pay Stephen his promised fee without dipping into the ever dwindling reserves of my extremely limited venture capital.

I sighed philosophically, realised that there wasn't anything I could do about it at this late stage, and settled back to watch the show.

Stephen is a pacer. Some mediums take a position centre stage and remain rooted to the spot all night. Not so this clairvoyant! He strides up and down the stage like a caged leopard, sometimes giving the impression that he is addressing the audience at large, other times seemingly talking to every person in the theatre on a purely individual basis.

'Ladies and gentlemen, what you are about to see isn't a show or a cabaret, it's a demonstration – a demonstration of clairvoyance! It's an experiment, which each and everyone of you is a part of! My name is Stephen Holbrook. I'm a spiritualist and it is my belief that you cannot die! Certainly there is a point in life when it's time for the spirit to pass on from the host body, and when that happens the *body* dies, but the *spirit* continues, maintaining its identity and its links with its loved ones from an afterlife in an other dimension. Some people call this other dimension "heaven" though whether it is or not I don't know because I haven't been there yet – ' a laugh ripples round the theatre ' – but I *do* know that there are spirits all around us, sending out messages of love and encouragement, and what I'm going to try and do this evening is act as a kind of telephone exchange between this world and those spirits who are trying to get messages across from the other side.

'Sometimes it's very difficult to know exactly what the spirits are trying to say, so I need you to help me as much as you can. If I come to you with a message I need to hear your voice – just a nice clear yes or no – please don't just sit there nodding your head because with all these spotlights shining in my eyes I probably won't see you, and it's actually the *sound* of your voice that enables me to make the link with the spiritual vibration.

'Every one got that? Good!' He takes a sip of water from the glass on the table next to him. ' – Then let's get started and see what we can do!'

More pacing. Long aggressive strides back and forth along the front of the apron, head down, fingers of his right hand clicking with impatience while the whole of his left arm has become unusually stiff, the left hand constricted into an arthritic claw...

'Don't worry about the arm,' he reassures us. 'This is just my spirit guide taking over...' And then after a few more seconds he stops mid-stride over towards the left of the stage and peers down with concentration into the front rows of the stalls.

'I want to be somewhere over here, a lady three or four rows back, who has lost her husband in the last two years... This gentleman would have passed over very suddenly with massive chest pains – ' Stephen shudders slightly and places his right hand over his heart. 'He wouldn't have been very old, only in his forties, and although he passed over with a heart attack, there would have been no previous indication of any kind of heart problem. Can anyone take this please?'

'I think this is me!' A lady in a green coat tentatively raises her hand, and sure enough, she's sitting in the third row of the stalls. Stephen picks her up immediately.

'Hello my love – now I just need your voice, nice and clear with a yes or no – this gentleman I have with me, very tall and straight, wearing glasses – wants me to tell you about *your* eyes – so can I ask you, have you been having some problems with your eyes?'

'Yes, I have.'

'And have you been *particularly* worried about your eyesight lately?'

'I suppose so, yes.'

'But you haven't actually been for an eye test, have you? I know you've been thinking about it, but you keep putting it off!'

'Yes, that's true...'

'Well the gentleman I've got with me is telling me to tell you to go and see an optician, for no other reason than to put your mind at rest. This gentleman is telling me you've got nothing to worry about, but you need to find this out for yourself. You need a new prescription, especially for your left eye, and this will sort out the headaches you've been having recently. Do you understand this, my love?'

'Yes. Yes I do.'

'I've got a name here... Does the name Maurice mean anything to you?'

'Yes, that was my husband's name.'

'...And tying in with Maurice I'm seeing railway lines and trains, so did Maurice work on the railways?'

The lady in green laughs a little bitterly. 'No, but he filled our attic with his silly model trains.'

Stephen relaxes a little. Thus far he has been quite tense. 'I've got something else here for you, my love... Maurice seems to be surrounded by dogs! Does *this* mean anything to you?'

'Oh yes. He worked for the RSPCA and he was a dog warden for the council...'

'Ummm, but would there have been one dog in particular that was very important, not just to Maurice, but to you as well? A very large shaggy dog, a bit like an Alsatian, but with long hair?'

'Oh yes, that would be Bruno,' the lady says warmly. 'He was a crossbred German Shepherd, and he got knocked over by a car about three years ago.'

'And does the name Tom or Tommy mean anything to you?'

'Tom? Tommy?' The lady sounds puzzled. 'No, I'm sorry, I don't think so...'

'Fine, thank you my love, can I say goodnight and God Bless? Just remember what Maurice has told you and do please make an appointment to see an optician, and I promise it will put your mind at rest... But now I've got to move on to someone called Tom or Tommy and I want to link Tom with someone called Dorothy, but my problem is I don't know which way round it is... Is there someone in the theatre called Tom who has a link with someone called Dorothy in spirit, or is there someone here called Dorothy who can link with Tom in spirit?'

There is a pregnant silence that lasts three seconds too long to be comfortable, then a male voice booms out from the back of the auditorium in a broad West Yorkshire accent.

'Ay lad, mah name's Tom an' me Mam died last year, but 'er name were Dotty not Dorothy.'

15

'But she would have been Christened Dorothy?' Stephen shoots back, trying to locate the voice at the rear of the building.

'Oh ay, but we never called 'er that.'

'Well I've got your Mum with me now sir and she's telling me that she never liked the name Dotty and that over there on the other side she's called Dorothy. She's also telling me something about the month of October – was there a birthday or anniversary in October?'

'She died in October. Two year ago as last year.'

'Thank you – ' Stephen slows down again, his words becoming hesitant, searchingly cautious. ' – Sir, would I be right in thinking that your Mum was a very large lady?'

'Ay, she were that all right!'

' – And would she have been on some very strong medication during the latter years of her life down here?'

'Ay, she were...'

Stephen doesn't give him time to finish. 'Sir, was your Mother diabetic?'

'Ay lad, she were!'

'And did she go into hospital about a month before she passed over? It would have been something to do with the diabetes, but she's telling me that she knew she wouldn't be coming out of that hospital once she'd gone in... I think she must have been in a coma or on life support for at least ten days before she finally slipped away – '

'Ay, just under a fortnight, it were...'

'And she's telling me that you were actually at her bedside holding her hand at the time of her passing! Everyone else had gone home at the end of visiting hours, *but you knew she wouldn't last the night* and you stayed until the very end!'

'Ah did that...' The big Yorkshireman's voice is husky and choked with emotion and you could hear a pin drop in the hushed and hallowed hall of the theatre.

'Well Tom your Mum just wants to say thank you because it was you more than the others who did most for her

16

in those last few years of her life. She knows she didn't thank you properly then, so she just wants to put the record straight and do it now. She's also telling me to tell you to stop worrying about Mark and Andrew... Sir, do you know who she's talking about here?'

'Ay, Mark an' Andy are me sons!'

'Well she's telling you to stop worrying and that everything will be sorted out by the end of the summer. She thinks it's a great idea for Mark and Andrew to go into business together, although she's well aware that you've had more than just a few doubts.'

'Ay, y'could say that. In fact, it's puttin' it mildly, like.'

'Well don't worry Tom, your boys will do well, and what's this about the sum of four thousand pounds... Tom, I'm getting the sum of four thousand pounds... This must mean something to you?'

'Ay, I've just forked out four grand for the little buggers to buy a car with... Goin' into taxi business, so they say!'

'Your Mum says it's a great idea and you'll have your cash back by the end of the year... Now, I'm picking up a young man who was killed violently in a road crash and he's telling me it would have been just before Christmas...'

Tom sounds baffled. 'No lad, dunno nowt about that...'

'Let's throw it open then... A young man, still only in his twenties, a road crash involving a motorbike and a car... The accident happened at night, and he wants to talk to.... Sandra? Is there a Sandra here tonight?'

'Me! *Me!* Over here!' A blond girl with a red leather top and a full metal jacket make-up job is actually standing up and waving excitedly at the stage.

'All right, my love, I've got you... Just hang on a minute while I tune in properly... Now I've got someone called Brian here with me... Is that right, my love? Was Brian killed in a road accident between a car and a motor bike, and would I be right in thinking that it was just before Christmas,

17

and would I also be right in thinking that it was Brian who was riding the bike?'

'Yes, yes to everything!' The girl is still standing, clenching and unclenching her fists, and her voice is on the edge of hysteria. She is obviously in a state of profound emotional distress, and an older woman has stood up next to her, wrapping a protective arm around her shoulders.

'Brian has a message for you,' Stephen says kindly. 'He wants you to know that he loves you very much and *that it wasn't his fault!* He really wants me to press home this point because he knows you've all been wondering about what exactly happened, and he wants you to know that the whole truth didn't come out at the inquest. He says that he didn't have a chance. The car came out of a side street without any lights and hit him broadside on. He says he didn't know he'd passed over until he was floating in the air above the wreckage. He says he wasn't ready to go, but he didn't feel any pain, and he's happy to stay where he is now, although he does miss you very much. He's also telling me about the yellow rose you put at his headstone on the day of the funeral, and he thanks you for it! Does this make any sense to you my love?'

'Oh yes, yes...' Sandra is openly crying now. 'All of it. Every word.'

'And you *did* put a yellow rose on his grave, the day of the funeral?'

'Yes, I did!'

'And what is the link between Brian and country and western music?'

'He was a professional musician and all he ever played was country and western!'

'He's telling me that you've got something important that belonged to him – it's hanging on your bedroom wall – and he wants to thank you for looking after Thin Lizzie for him... Can you link with all of this?'

'Yes, Thin Lizzie was his favourite guitar, and you're right, it's hanging on my bedroom wall...'

'And who is Edna?'

'I am,' calls out the older woman standing next to Sandra.

'Okay. Let's see if I've got this right. Sandra, you were Brian's fiancée?'

'Yes...' The word is lost in a sob.

'In that case, Edna, you're Brian's Mum?'

'Yes.'

'Right... Brian's telling me something about the number 23 – Does this mean anything to either of you?'

'He died on the 23rd of December.' Edna's voice conveys a sense of disbelief at the statement that she herself has just made. Stephen now moves to the very edge of the stage and hunkers down on his haunches. His voice drops to a low conversational tone, but even from the back of the balcony I can hear every word that he says.

'Brian wants you to know that although he was always a bit of a loner when he was down here on this plane, he isn't alone any more. He's got a lot of friends with him now, and he's telling me about Pete and Ted and Jack... Do these names mean anything to you, my love?'

'Pete was his best friend. He got killed two years ago, also on a motorbike. Ted and Jack were Brian's father and brother.'

'And would I be right in thinking that when they were down here together, Brian and Ted and Jack never got on very well together?'

'No they didn't.' Edna sounds very fragile. 'In fact, they used to fight like cat and dog...'

'Well they're not fighting now,' Stephen says emphatically. 'They know you've suffered a terrible triple loss in the last few years, and they know how hard it has been for you. They're telling you and Sandra that you've got to struggle on and make the best of things, and that they are all together now and they'll be doing their best to help as much as they can from the other side. So can I leave you with that? Goodnight and God Bless and thank you very much!'

Stephen moved on to forge another link, and in fact brought over another dozen messages during the course of the rest of the evening. He talked to a woman about her late mother, named the lady's name and even named the hospital where she'd passed over. He linked in with somebody's Grandfather who had been a bomber pilot in the last war, and brought through a very poignant message from a little girl who had died of leukaemia when she was only six years old...

To be honest, I don't remember all of the details. I had taped the first three links, but had only brought the tape recorder as an 11th hour afterthought and hadn't checked the batteries. Needless to say the damn thing ground to a sluggish halt just as Stephen was moving on from Sandra and Edna.

Even so, I *do* remember the shape of the evening – the pin dropping silences and the moments of awe and breathless anticipation on the part of the audience, caused by the raw naked human emotion of the event.

From a purely professional stand point I was enormously impressed by Stephen's demonstration, and on a personal level, in a very odd way, I was strangely disturbed by the strength and detail of his evidence. When I later tried to analyse my feelings, I recognised that I had been both humbled and moved.

As an interesting footnote to this chapter, once Stephen realised that we had not taken enough cash to cover his fee, he refused point blank to take any money for his services that night. I argued like mad, but he would have none of it – and I was left with no choice other than to take this as a gesture of his tremendous generosity. He later confided in me that he felt he was being guided by spirit, and as we both came to realise in the fullness of time, there were reasons within reasons for this act of sympathetic goodwill.

20

Chapter Three: The Great Zareada

The road from Ilkley to York meanders and twists – there are no short cuts and the complicated 32 mile trip can sometimes feel like 320. But that night as I drove home from Stephen's demonstration I felt out of time and place; I had no real impression of the journey and I think the old red Volvo navigated itself home on auto pilot. The "disturbed" feeling was persistent, and beneath it there was a curious brisance of something which came very close to anger.

Anger?

Yes, on the face of it rather an odd emotion in the circumstances – why, for heaven's sake, should I be feeling angry? When I focused inwards and analysed my innermost thoughts and feelings, I came to recognise that although there was no *simple* explanation for the mood, there *were* explanations – but to find them I would have to turn the clock back almost forty years to the beginning of another association with a clairvoyant medium. His name was Ossie Rae, but in most circles he was better known as The Great Zareada.

It was 1961 and I was fourteen years old. My mind twists through the avenues of time and I realise that I am looking back on a different world. The Second World War, ended a scant sixteen years earlier, was still fresh in the consciousness of the nation and the *cold* war was freezing us with the worry of a nuclear holocaust. John F. Kennedy was the newly inaugurated president of The United States and Nikita Khrushchev was thinking that it might be a good idea to dispatch a few ICBM's to Cuba. The Beatles had begun to invoke the phenomenon of Beatlemania, and a Rolling Stone was something other than a brick that gathered no moss.

Hari Krishna had yet to arrive on the streets of London and the "sixties" had a long way to go before they really started to swing. Cigarettes cost two shillings (10p) for twenty and the same two shillings would buy you a gallon of four star on most filling station forecourts – except in those days filling stations were unique to America and we still topped up our tanks at the local garage.

1961 was much *much* closer to 1945 than it is to 2001, and not just chronologically, but also culturally and socially! The youth revolution was still an embryonic and unfocused mood of rebellion finding its first unsteady feet in rock and roll music and I suppose that I was in the vanguard of that revolution, for even at fourteen years old I was already earning a reasonable living as a pop singer – which brings me directly to Ossie Rae and The Great Zareada.

The summer of 1961 saw me in a revue show in the small seaside town of Whitby in North Yorkshire – my mother, the original 'lady of the theatre' was third on the bill, and she'd dragged me along to prop up the bottom. The so called top of the bill was the Geordie comedian Tommy Bradley, but it was The Great Zareada who pulled in the punters.

Looking back on it now this was a beautiful world of youth and colour, the excitement of "curtain up", the unforgettable smell of Leichener's 5 and 9 greasepaint, the camaraderie of theatre people in cramped dressing rooms... I wrote my first poems, strummed my first chords, and discovered girls in the form of Shirley Jangles, called so because of the enormous jangling charm bracelets she wore, one on each wrist. There were Bonny Sue, June and Geraldine, and there were Alyson and Jane... These were the other five chorus girls, but it was Shirley Jangles who caused my knees to tremble and who was responsible for that hollow pit of nervous tension in the soul of my stomach.

It was in the Summer of 1961 that I did my first serious drinking in pubs and low life taverns that I had no legal right to visit, bought my first packets of cigarettes (Players Gold Leaf in the distinctive red and white box) and discovered that it was not only *girls* who liked boys! (A couple of narrow

22

escapes, but it was a useful learning curve, and I soon recognised who I could trust and who were the odd bods to avoid.)

I had my first taste of recognition with people smiling at me and waving to me in the street on the strength of their visit to the theatre the night before, and for the first time in my life I was earning a proper fee rather than just pocket money.

At fourteen I honestly did not know a single thing about clairvoyancy or spiritualism – to be sure, my fey old grandmother had tried to teach me the rudiments of palmistry and the tarot, but this was a far far cry from what Ossie Rae did for his living.

With hindsight I recognise that I may have been an impressionable fourteen year old and I further recognise that my memory might not be as accurate as I might like to assume, but even so, Ossie Rae *did* make an impression, and night after night I watched him from the wings of the theatre marvelling at what he did, wanting to know how he did it, and desperately wanting (for all the wrong reasons) to be able to do it myself. If *I* could do what *he* could do, what a difference that might make in my quest for Shirley Jangles!

Off stage, Ossie was a large fat man with thick black wavy hair and not a tooth in his mouth. He was blatantly gay (which might explain his interest in me although he never once, in all the years I knew him, made any kind of overture or advance towards me.) He drank sparingly, but smoked heavily – a forty a day man, twenty Kingsway and twenty Consulate – and he had a ribald and expressive sense of humour which took high camp into new realms of theatricality.

On stage The Great Zareada was a different person entirely. Superbly fitted suit that disguised his girth, hair swept back á la Elvis Presley, but with two streaks of silver grey sprayed on at the temples – and, of course, a set of gleaming white dentures made a huge difference! His act was simplicity itself – he would send a tray around the audience, and while some volunteer, usually from the front of the stalls, would supervise the fitting of a black velvet blindfold over roundels of cotton wool and plasticine, the audience would be invited to place personal items on the tray. The tray would come back to the stage, and one at a time he'd take an item from the tray, tune in to the owners voice... "Just a simple yes or no, please" – and then proceed to deliver a devastatingly accurate and highly detailed clairvoyant reading using the relatively rare gift of psychometry.

He named names, was quite specific about dates and anniversaries, took on health conditions to the extent that he could tell someone exactly when a loved one had passed over and what had been the cause of their passing – how long they'd taken to go, who had attended the funeral, who had been absent, and why! There was never hint, innuendo or allusion. Ossie's evidence was hard, detailed and factual, even down to the minutiae of detail... If, for example, he had a link with somebody's father, he would give the man's name, describe him accurately, not only physically, but also in character; he would describe specific objects that belonged to the man – a car (a Morris Minor) a horse (fifteen hands called Northboy) a watch (a pocket hunter, made of silver, inscribed "with love from Flora to Frank, Montreal 1939") – he would further describe other people in life that the departed would have known, accurately assessing the various relationships. He was able to link in with time and death circumstances... "Your husband was killed in April – April the 13th 1943 – he was shot down in a Wellington bomber over the German city of Essen, and he was the navigator of the aircraft... Please tell me, Madam, is this information correct?" Inevitably the answer would be yes, but he'd seldom let it go at that.... "....of course, you didn't receive the telegram until May 22nd, and even then, it wasn't until four years later that you yourself went to the trouble to discover exactly what happened to Frank on that dreadful April night...'

24

Ossie, who was a close pal of my Mother, was not a flash in the pan of my life, and although I may have been impressionable in 1961 I was less so in 1963, 1964, 1968, 1971, 1973, and 1975 which were all periods in which I was either on tour or in a summer show with him: whether it was in the cabaret clubs of the North, small provincial theatres, holiday camps or up-market restaurants, I must have watched many thousands of his demonstrations, and although obviously he had his off nights, by and large, his evidence was always detailed, concise, direct and provable.

There was another side to Ossie's life of which the paying public was seldom aware. For example, few Sundays would pass without Ossie taking a service in a spiritualist church, and he did an incredible amount of free work, either for charities or for people who needed his help. On more than one occasion in his varied career he was of invaluable help to the police, and he was a key player in resolving the mystery of the Spennymoor murders back in the 1950's. He pampered to the gay side of his nature by playing pantomime dame for anyone who would give him a job, and although he was seldom out of work, he was never overtly wealthy. He had an ongoing hate quest against stage magicians (a gentleman called Maurice Fogel in particular) but his sense of humour and his sense of spirit were indomitable.

Ossie always amazed and surprised, and it is little wonder that he stimulated admiration and intrigue within my young man's soul. On more than one occasion I would watch him walk across a room and four feet before he got to the door the door would open for him, seemingly of its own accord, and then close quietly behind him after he passed through the portal. I remember quizzing him about this and his explanation was simple: "I think I do a lot to help spirit and every now and again spirit says thank you by showing me some small courtesy." This may sound immodest and, for all I know, it may not have been an accurate assessment of the phenomenon, but the way in which he said it was not immodest, and it is certainly what *he* believed.

Ossie Zareada Rae deserves a book of his own, and maybe one day someone will write it, but *this* book is about Stephen Holbrook, and although I have allowed myself to get sidetracked, there is a very good reason for it.

I remember a pantomime season in Bishop Auckland. It was Christmas Eve, no-one had been paid for the rehearsal week, so rather than shelling out cash that we didn't have on digs, we'd all dossed down in the dressing rooms in an attempt to save some money. It was freezing cold and our Christmas fayre consisted of sandwiches, thermos flasks of coffee, and a small Christmas pudding, which Ossie spent three hours trying to cook in a tin can suspended above half a dozen candles. It was a funny but frustrating process.

'Do you know,' I remember him saying with a giggle, 'I'll go to my death cooking bloody Christmas pud!' And exactly twenty years later, while cooking another Christmas pudding, he collapsed and died with a cerebral haemorrhage – and a bright and incandescent spark flickered out from this world of blood and tears.

Long before Ossie's death I had become totally fascinated by spiritualism and clairvoyance, and sometimes with his guidance although more often on my own, I delved into this world, researching, exploring and learning as much as I could from whatever sources I could find.

It became apparent quite early on that I myself was devoid of spiritual sight – by all means, I could read a palm and make sense of a complicated tarot spread, and came to acknowledge that I had some psychic ability – but this was not what I wanted, was not what I was searching for. It was the essence of spirit that was missing. I knew that the spirit was there – I'd seen it in Ossie's work and had read about it in a dozen books, and had even experienced it in another form in my experiments with magic and the occult, for if a well crafted spell worked then a spiritual prayer by necessity had to have been answered – *but this was still not the same thing!*

After Ossie died I went about the business of finding a new guru and thus began a long slow process of disillusionment. I visited scores of self-styled clairvoyants and saw dozens of pretenders strutting their stuff on various stages. Even the so called "star names" of the psychic world seemed to offer only the flimsiest of evidence drawn from conjecture and clever guesswork, and although I benefited indirectly from these experiences in the sense of learning what not to do myself if I was reading somebody's palm or tarot cards ("Always tell but never ask") I realised that Ossie had set a benchmark that no-one else had ever come anywhere close to... That is, until Stephen Holbrook came along!

Ossie must have been in his late fifties when he passed over, and although Stephen was not quite as detailed or as specific as Ossie had been with his evidence, it had to be remembered that Stephen was still only in his early thirties. With another twenty years experience and development, what new doors might he open, what old benchmarks might he surpass? Harry Andrews had used Doris Stokes as *his* benchmark, but in my opinion (and no offence to Doris) Stephen was by far the stronger clairvoyant.

I was angry that it had taken me the better part of twenty years to find someone approaching Ossie's plane of spiritual cohesion, and stupidly I was angry with Stephen himself! Where had he been all this time and why had he been hiding from me? I was angry with myself for not having looked harder.

But beyond the anger there was a turbulent wellspring of excitement and exultation. Ossie had answered many of my questions as best he could, but I realised that I had not always asked the right questions and had not always heeded nor fully understood some of the answers. My interest in spiritualism had dwindled into cynicism – Ossie had offered the seeds of great knowledge and understanding, but had passed over before the fruits had ripened. In search of those fruits from other sources I had become disillusioned and disappointed, but now, with this new association with Stephen Holbrook, my old interests were suddenly rekindled with a fire of fresh enthusiasm and I felt that if I asked the right questions I might start getting some of the right answers – answers that were significantly more important now that I was in my fifties and no longer the angsty impatient young man I'd been in my shallow twenties.

Driving on auto-pilot back to York, not registering the traffic lights in Otley or the switching S bends that took me through Pool and Arthington and only marginally aware of the driving rain that cascaded against the windscreen, I was filled with a deep sense of rightness and inevitability and deep down in the very seat of my soul I just *knew* that there was some greater point and purpose to my association with Stephen than I could even begin to put into words... But even so, I also knew that his arrival in my life was most timely.

Chapter Four: In The Beginning

Stephen was born at a very early age and spent most of his childhood growing up. In many respects he was a very ordinary little boy full of fun and mischief, while at the same time being quite sensitive and sometimes over emotional. Even in the arms of a very safe family environment, he sometimes experienced the need for solitude.

Given the close bonds with his parents and two doting sisters, it might seem a little odd that he should have forged such a strong link with his Grandfather, John – but it is something of a curiosity that clairvoyant children, whether they are aware of their gifts or not, do seem to enjoy separate, and usually quite powerful relationships with one or more of their grandparents.

As Stephen toddled through his infant years, moving through his primary education at Walton Village School just outside his native Wakefield, there was no hint of any kind of psychic activity or any indication of what was to come a little while later. His young world revolved around his schoolwork, his family and his friends, and in particular his rather unusual relationship with Granddad John.

To all intents and purposes Stephen's Grandfather seems to have been a rather unorthodox character, a rebel within the framework of his own time and society: garrulous, eccentric, funny and humorous, generous to a fault but at the same time incredibly canny and careful with his money to the point of occasionally coming over as the archetypal penny pinching Yorkshire Tyke.

During a period in which Stephen's father managed the highly prestigious Wakefield Theatre Club, Stephen and his Granddad would frequently wander around the premises the morning after a night before, perhaps on the pretext of helping the cleaners, but more certainly to gather up the discarded fag ends that John would then break up and re-roll at his leisure. Frequently John and Stephen would share a fish and chip supper, but if there was any left in the newspaper, rather than being discarded, it would be kept in the 'fridge overnight and reheated for the following day's lunch!

Like a leading character from "Last Of The Summer Wine" Stephen's Grandfather made a profound impression, and when Stephen speaks of him today, he does so with obvious love and deep affection.

'I suppose,' he muses in reflection, 'that one of the reasons why Granddad seems so important to me now, even after all these years, is that he played such a pivotal role in my life while I was still just a child. I remember that when I was seven years old I came face to face with death for the first time, and it changed my life in an instant...

'Granddad had this dog, a big black loppy hound, and I'd take it for long walks around the outskirts of the village, although I suppose the dog was far too strong for me to control. Anyway, on this one particular day, it pulled the lead out of my hand to dash across the road after a rabbit or something, and it promptly got run over and killed by a car. I can't tell you how upset I was. One minute the dog was there, woofing and frolicking and so full of life, the next minute it was dead and silent and covered with blood...

'I know that I was deeply upset about this for ages and ages. Until the dog got killed I'd never seen death, never even thought about it. I'd just assumed that the people we loved, whether they've got four legs or only two, would always be there with us, and it was a dreadful shock to discover that this wasn't the case.'

In the early 1980's Stephen's Grandfather became very seriously ill and the family steeled itself to face the impending loss. This, of course, was something not known by Stephen himself. As far as he was concerned "Granddad was poorly in hospital" but it had never crossed his mind that his Grandfather might be *terminally* ill, and remembering the fact that Stephen was only in his very early teens, it is quite understandable that the family, still hoping for some last minute remission, would have kept the hard core of probable truth from him.

Stephen remembers waking up in the middle of the night and being quite surprised to find his Grandfather sitting on the end of the bed. 'Yes, I suppose I was a bit surprised,' he recalls, 'but I wasn't frightened or anything. This was my Granddad, wearing his favourite purple cardigan. When I asked him what he was doing here in the middle of the night, he gave me the most enormous smile, and told me that he'd just popped in to say goodbye, and that I should close my eyes and go back to sleep. So I closed my eyes, but then opened them again straight away, and Granddad wasn't there any more. Now *this* made me upset, and I started to cry, although I wasn't quite sure why I was crying. I remember looking at the alarm clock and seeing that it was still only just four o'clock in the morning...

'I suppose I must have dozed off, but I woke up again at the usual time to start getting ready for school. I felt a bit tired and fed up, and when my Mum asked me what was wrong with me, I remember telling her that I'd had this visit from Granddad at four o'clock in the morning – for some reason I found I didn't really want to talk about it – and although she didn't pursue the matter, I do recall that she did give me a very funny look...

'Anyway, I left for school at half past eight and at five minutes to nine my Mum had a phone call from the local hospital to say that Granddad had passed away in his sleep and the time on the death certificate was given as 3.55 AM.'

It is not uncommon for departing souls to visit their loved ones at the time of death. This is a well-documented phenomenon, and indeed I myself have had some first hand experience of this situation. From Stephen's point of view, however, this was the first clearly defined, proven and well corroborated association with psychism and the world of

31

spirit and it seems to have acted as a catalyst for everything which came afterwards.

What do you do when a loved one dies? How do you cope with the loss? How do you fill the void? How do you do it when you're still only a child? Different people have different techniques and remedies, but basically what we all do is swallow our grief, gird our loins and get on with the business of life as best we can. In this respect, young Stephen and his family were just like the rest of us, but in Stephen's own words 'after Granddad went my life was never quite the same again. I missed him then and I still miss him now.'

As Stephen progressed through his teens his schoolwork began to suffer. It seemed that he could not concentrate on any of the lessons, and indeed many a school report stated quite bluntly "Stephen is a bright boy but suffers from a marked absence of concentration."

What is interesting is the *cause* of this absence of concentration. 'It was sometimes very difficult to hear what the teachers were saying. There were other voices in my head, a babble of words that were there more as thoughtforms than actually spoken words. I didn't know where the words were coming from, and I certainly didn't know what they were saying. There were times when I thought I was going mad, but I didn't want to tell anyone else about what was happening to me in case they thought I was going mad too. There would be times when the babble of voices would be still and quiet for a while, but sooner or later they always came back, and when they did, they were always more strident and insistent than they had been before.'

Listening to Stephen tell this story now, I marvel that he managed to survive his school days at all. Few kids, especially in these later years of academic education where there is a sustained force-feeding of facts designed to get them through specific exams with grades that are a credit to the school if not to the child, find the educational process easy. In Stephen's case he was working with a profound handicap and it is all credit to his resourcefulness and determination that he got grades as good as he did. By his own admission they were not *good* grades, but they got him through, albeit at a price.

At 16 years old Stephen took the brave and unprecedented step of going to see his local doctor. 'I had to do something! The voices in my head were becoming unbearable. I couldn't sleep properly, I wasn't eating and I couldn't think straight. I thought I might be having some sort of nervous breakdown, so I reckoned that if I could get some tranquillisers or something, I might be able to turn things around a bit.'

Now you could say that God looks after his own, or you could just say that Stephen was extremely lucky in his choice of doctor. What is fairly clear is the fact that most doctors would either have prescribed the requested tranquillisers or passed their patient on for some kind of psychiatric assessment... Stephen's GP, a much more enlightened soul, listened to everything Stephen had to say, before offering a prescription.

'I think,' said the good doctor, 'that before I start filling your system with drugs, you should pay a visit to Peterson Road.'

'Er, yes, of course,' young Stephen stammered in response, 'but what's at Peterson Road?'

'The local spiritualist church,' the doctor had replied soberly. ' – But there's just one thing, if you *do* decide to pay them a visit, don't tell anyone that I sent you!'

Chapter Five: The Spiritualist Church

If we look at spiritualism from a purely philosophical standpoint then it is arguably one of the oldest religions in the world, not only drawing eclectically on every other world faith, but more importantly providing those faiths with the cornerstones of their respective beliefs, i.e. that (a) there is a spiritual afterlife of one form or another and that (b) what we do down here on this earth plane of existence influences in no small way what we may find in that afterlife.

If, however, we look at spiritualism as a world religion, it differs from every other faith insofar as it offers tangible proof of a spiritual afterlife. The Christian Church dictates "you must have blind faith and as for the proof, well just take our word for it" whereas The Spiritualist Church says "here is some hard evidence for life after death, now go and build your own faith on the strength of the evidence."

Little wonder that the established Christian Church has always been virulently hostile towards the spiritualist movement, (as indeed it has to anything which has threatened its monopoly over the spiritual enlightenment and welfare of the population at large) and this despite the fact that the early founders of the Spiritualist Church in the United Kingdom came from strong Christian backgrounds! Indeed, one of the key personalities within the early church was the Reverend Stainton Moses, who was at one and the same time a Christian clergyman, a Theosophist and a practising medium.

In the UK, spiritualism is relatively modern religion. Finding its foundations in the mid 19th century, it is loosely based on the much older French sect of Spiritism which grew prolifically in Europe during the 16th and 17th centuries, going on to become the second most practised religion in Brazil after Roman Catholicism.

As far as this country is concerned three Davids – David Richmond, David Weatherall and David Wilkinson convened a gathering of what they called The First Spiritualist Church in Darlington in 1853 and later in the same year the church was officially founded in Keighly. It is interesting to note that despite later enthusiasm from the aristocracy and intelligentsia in London and the South, initially this was a strongly working class movement founded in the very roots of the North.

All three of the Davids were secularists and rationalists and David Richmond was a non-conformist shaker with his roots firmly planted in the philosophies of Engels and other Utopian visionaries. The philosophy of the Spiritualist Church or, if you like, its mission statement, has remained constant throughout its existence to this present day. It advocates post mortem survival of the spirit, moral responsibility of the individual, the Fatherhood of God and the Brotherhood of Man, and the Ministry of Angels.

Its stance is totally non-doctrinal, and it welcomes people from all other faiths regardless of race, creed or culture. Indeed it is not uncommon to find traditional Christians, dedicated Moslems and devout Jews among the ranks and congregations of The Spiritualist Church, holding, as it were, dual allegiance to the single throne of God. As with Islam, The Spiritualist Church accepts the life and teachings of Jesus Christ as a great healer and teacher, even as *a* Son of God, though perhaps not *the only* Son of God.

From my own personal observations made over the last thirty years or so, and confirmed by friends and associates who have a far more active role in the movement than I do, one clearly defined and unofficial ethos of the church is its non evangelical stance. No one in the spiritualist faith is saying that you "should" do this, or you've "got" to do that or you "can't" do the other. The concept of individual moral responsibility is cut deep into the bedrock of its foundation. There is little or no patronisation, and by and large the congregations are drawn from ordinary people (and some quite *extra*ordinary people) from all walks of life.

Over the years the movement has had its highs and lows, but right now many of the congregations are in a state of unprecedented growth. In the city of York, for example, membership of the local centre has risen from 17 to 210 just in the last five years, with a significant number of younger people swelling the ranks.

One might cynically attribute this to the rise of New Age awareness prevalent within our society during the latter years of the 20th Century, but one might just as easily argue in favour of an enhancement of the overall spiritual vibration that is making people search for something tangible upon which to hang their religious beliefs. The Christian Church's traditional dogma of "you must have faith" is no longer good enough for a new generation of individuals brought up with TV sound bytes and computer wizardry. Today's thinking individual demands answers and believes that he has a right to those answers: in the same way that he is dubious about the truthfulness of any politician's statement or political position, he is also dubious about The Christian Church's belief that the only pathway to the House of God is through the teachings of Jesus of Nazareth.

I suspect that these are the factors, along with The Spiritualist Church's unique ability to facilitate communication (albeit far from perfect communication) between this world and the afterlife, that are responsible for the current upsurge of interest in the spiritualist movement.

One contact within the church has told me that the current renaissance of interest is reminiscent of what he called "the golden early days" of the movement during the terrible blood soaked years of the First World War.

Britain's young men were dying in their hundreds of thousands and the psycho-emotional shock to the nation, both on a conscious and subliminal level, was without precedent. Mothers, fathers and wives flocked to spiritualist meetings all over the country, no doubt reassured by the endorsement of people like Sir Arthur Conan Doyle, who was not only a totally committed supporter of the movement but also the most popular novelist and writer of his generation.

In later years the Spiritualist Church suffered and struggled: there were too many frauds and exposés and there were never enough funds. Congregations fell dramatically and there is a stereotyped image of a few odd bods huddled together in draughty back street halls, determined in their conviction and despairingly trying to keep their faith alive. This stereotype is reasonably accurate and certainly reflects my own visits to various meetings up and down the country during the 60's, 70's and 80's. There is no doubt that there *has* been a renaissance during the 1990's, perhaps because of the points I made earlier, perhaps because there has been a re-emergence of physical mediumship, and perhaps because during the last ten or twelve years the movement has done a great deal to modernise itself. A few of the tatty back street halls do still remain, but increasingly there are many bright new centres and a new breed of stewardship at the helm of the movement, which unfettered by the dogma of other faiths, is able to reach out through modern mediums of communication such as the Internet, and make contact with spiritual people all over the globe. This is neither cynical nor aggressive, and it is not evangelical – but it is an excellent example of how ultra modern technology can be used to spread the good word of a very old message.

Stephen Holbrook became a member of the Spiritualist Church in the mid 1980's. He was immediately at his ease and through sitting in development circles was able to start controlling the babble of voices that had plagued his head for such a long time. These voices, he was told, were spirit voices trying to make contact with the earth plane, and because through quirk of genes, DNA or serendipity, Stephen was a natural clairaudient medium, it was inevitable that the voices should home in on the psychic signal that, unbeknown to him, he had been emitting since childhood.

Chapter Six: The Early Years

Within the fellowship of the Spiritualist Church Stephen was able to relax and claw back some sense of normality into his life.   In his school years the babbling voices, frequently presenting themselves as disjointed thoughtforms rather than actual words, had been a chaotic jumble of extra sensory perception which had frequently threatened to overload the young clairvoyant's developing psyche and the regular flashes of precognition had been more alarming than revealing.

Now, at Peterson Road, Stephen learned how to mute the voices, how to tune in and listen to what they were saying. Some semblance of order was drawn into the cacophony of psychic noise as he learned how to focus his powers of precognition and make some sense of the sounds and visions he was hearing and seeing. It did not happen all at once, but over a couple of years a tremendous degree of progress was made.

As part of his training he would give free personal readings and always managed to impress his sitters with his perception and accuracy. It would be wrong to say that Stephen became blasé about his new life style, but now that the tension and ignorance had been removed, he was able to accept the tenets of spiritualism and get on with the business of being ordinary. For his own personal evidence he was always mindful of his Grandfather's nocturnal visit, and was able to embrace the idea of spirit world with an open heart and an equally open mind.

One very powerful and stabilising influence came in the form of his tentative teenage courtship with Caroline, who over the years graduated from the roles of childhood sweetheart to serious girlfriend, fiancé and ultimately into the much cherished position of becoming Stephen's wife. I think this must be another example of how spirit looks after its own, for in these turbulent days when relationships last as long as the next argument, Stephen and Caroline have sustained a successful union with three beautiful children as the natural result of their dedication and commitment to each other. Stephen says that 'even in the very early days she became my foundation stone, my focus point, my reason for being alive, and it's just the same now as it was back then.'

Even though still only in his mid-teens Stephen's reputation began to grow and he had no shortage of clients queuing up to sit at his table. He conducted private readings because he felt it was the right thing to do, but he never felt particularly happy confronting a sitter on a one to one basis. He puts this down to shyness and the responsibility of fulfilling his client's expectations. This pattern of working was soon to change, however, and one specific situation led directly to him moving away from doing private sittings to taking the public platform.

At that time Stephen's sister Joanne was dating a young man called Paul who was the resident DJ at Casanova's nightclub in Wakefield. Casanova's was one of the North's premier venues, and Paul's position within the hierarchy of the establishment was quite senior, and certainly to the extent that he knew what was going on in the club, even if it didn't involve him directly.

Paul arranged a sitting with Stephen, because unbeknown to our hero, a substantial sum of money had gone missing from the club's coffers, and Paul had the faint hope that Stephen might be able to throw some light on the subject. No one was under direct suspicion of having stolen the money, but its absence from its rightful place was casting a shadow over the venue and causing no small degree of friction and speculation among the staff.

Stephen picked up on a number of things that had nothing to do with the reason why Paul was consulting him, and Paul was "gobsmacked" when Stephen spoke of a young lady who had died in very strange circumstances ' – I see this young woman surrounded in sparkling light, but it isn't ordinary light, it's something like ultra violet light, the sort of light that comes off a sun bed… There's a tremendous sense of heat and dizziness, and this girl is telling me that it was all an accident and she didn't know what had happened until she woke up on the other side…'

Paul knew exactly what Stephen was talking about for only a few weeks earlier a friend had actually died while lying on a sun bed. She had fallen asleep beneath the UV lights, and sadly, perhaps because the sun beds of the 1980's were not the sophisticated pieces of equipment they are today, the system had shorted and she had been accidentally electrocuted.

Of course, if Stephen had known about this incident it would have made the whole reading a bit of a travesty. But the point is, he did *not* know! Paul, having been very distressed by his friend's death, had kept it very much to himself.

With regard to the missing cash, Stephen got to it eventually. He received the strong impression of lots of five and ten pound notes being swept over by rushing water in a dark and confined space…

This, it has to be said, made very little sense to Stephen, and to be truthful, at the time it didn't make too much sense to Paul either. But Stephen's words lingered in Paul's mind and when the club's management elected to do one more thorough search before calling in the police, Paul mentioned the curious message he had received from Stephen. This led to some hilarity, but much to everyone's surprise, they came across the cash wrapped in oilskins and stuffed beneath the drains… which to Paul's way of thinking was a clear confirmation of Stephen's vision. No one ever discovered who had stashed the missing money in such an obscure hiding place, but Paul and I share the same opinion that without Stephen's words providing the subconscious clue, it might still be stashed there to this very day.

40

When a visiting medium failed to show up as expected Paul immediately recommended Stephen to take her place, and thus with much trepidation, and still only seventeen years old, Stephen stepped out onto the public stage for the first time.

'How did you feel?' I asked him when we were talking about this a few weeks ago.

'Totally bloody petrified!' he laughed. 'I had *no* idea what was going to happen, what I was going to say or what I was going to do. It was an act of absolute faith. I knew most of the people in the room, and in one way that was good because if I fell on my arse I knew they'd be there to pick me up afterwards – but in another way it was totally intimidating and it might have been easier if I'd been facing a room full of strangers.'

'So what *did* happen?' I prompted him.

'Dunno,' he answered in his maddeningly vague way, 'but I must have been reasonably okay because that first night led to lots of other nights, not just at Peterson Road, but other churches and centres around the area...'

'Yes,' I insisted, 'but what actually happened, or if you like, what actually happens *today* when you walk out on to the stage and see your audience for the first time? Where do you start? How do you begin?'

'Oh that's easy,' he said. 'I'm still totally petrified but I just listen to the voices, go where they want me to go and say what they want me to say and it usually works out all right – doesn't it?'

Stephen is a lovely lovely man, but there are times, dear reader, when I want to wring his neck! I try to place myself in his shoes, try to imagine what it might be like walking out onto an empty stage, without any indication of what I might find when I get there – and I just can't do it!

With my own background I have walked onto a thousand stages and have never had a problem with nerves or stage fright, but that's because I've always known what I was going

41

to say and do, or when I was gigging, what songs I was going to sing. Certainly I might be a wee bit apprehensive about using somebody else's PA equipment, and occasionally I might worry a bit about a new set of guitar strings, but I've never had to walk onto a stage hoping that when I get there someone will hand me a well tuned guitar and a nicely balanced microphone. You check and double check everything, leaving as little as possible to chance, and knowing that within the framework of your own talent and experience you can deliver the goods. In Stephen's case, and by his own estimation of what happens, none of these guarantees or preparations are in place, and when *he* takes the stage it is an act of blind faith that all will be well. Just to think about it brings me, hardened performer that I am, out into a cold sweat!

It takes three or four years to train a nurse, five or six years to train a doctor, and about seven years to train a priest. It also takes around six or seven years to properly train a clairvoyant or clairaudient medium, even if the training regime is a somewhat softer process.

Between his sixteenth and twenty third year Stephen gently nurtured his gift with no shortage of help and support from both friends and family alike, and making a number of contacts with people who were destined to have a highly influential role in his later life, not least of which were Janet Fergussen and her extremely talented Grand-daughter, Jane McDonald, who both became ardent fans and the firmest of friends. He committed himself to a YTS course in hairdressing, and actually went on to become a professional hairdresser with his own salon in the centre of Leeds – which at the time of writing is still the case.

With his life in order, he was for a while quite satisfied with his lot, but increasingly in his early twenties he began to become just a little frustrated with the spiritualist church –

and particularly with some of the clairvoyant demonstrations he witnessed.

'I'd be sitting there, watching this or that visiting medium, and thinking to myself "no they've got that wrong, it isn't Sheila that's trying to get a message through, it's Sally," or "no you don't want to be talking to someone on the back row with this message, it's the lady down here in front of me with the blue hat," – and in the end I came to the conclusion that rather than sitting there watching other people either cock it up or only get it half right, I'd better have a go at it myself and see if I could do any better. I'd done lots of demonstrations around the local spiritualist churches, but honestly I was getting a bit negative about all the hymn singing and the prayers, and I wanted the whole thing to be brighter and more accessible, and I also wanted to talk to people who didn't know anything about spiritualism or who wouldn't be seen dead inside a spiritualist church. I'm not evangelical, but I did find myself thinking that if I was going to preach the message of life after death there wasn't much point in preaching to the converted.'

'So what did you do?' I asked.

'Took the bull by the horns, as it were, and booked myself into Morley Town Hall – an evening of clairvoyance with Stephen Holbrook, Yorkshire's Youngest Medium! I think about forty people turned up, and twenty of them were pals I'd conned into buying a ticket, but before I went on that night my hand was shaking so much I couldn't even hold a pint without spilling half of it down the front of my nice new shirt. I can't actually remember much about that first night, what I said or what messages came through or anything, but I do know that I was very relieved when it was all over. It was only afterwards, when I was going over things in my mind, that I realised that I had actually enjoyed myself, and much of this was due to the tremendous buzz I got from the audience. Anyway, that was the start of it, and I've just gone on from there…'

43

Stephen – on Stephen and Spiritualism

I need to tell you about a lady called Una Pearce. Ten years ago she was the main person I looked up to – and I still do, as a matter of fact. She is one of those people who gives everything to everyone with no gain for herself. She is a genuine medium and she was my inspiration. When I first saw her work I saw how accurate and how sincere she was with her evidence, I knew she was the right kind of person for me to model myself on.

I don't want to offend anyone but something I have noticed with other mediums is that the quality of their evidence is a bit wishy washy and if the spirit world is going to use us as channels of communication to give messages back to people in the audience or even in private sittings, they're going to come through with some hard evidence, something really worthwhile, to prove their existence... And this is where Una Pearce was absolutely brilliant!

Long before I ever met her, when I was just starting at Peterson Road, I phoned her up to try and make an appointment. She told me that she was far too busy to see me – but that she sensed that my Grandfather was with me and that he was telling her that I was wearing his ring, a ring with the initials JCS inscribed on it – but that the initials had rubbed off! This was quite correct! I was wearing Granddad's ring, he was called John Clifford Sykes, and the initials were quite worn, to the extent that you'd only be able to read them if you looked really hard. I thought "bloody hell, how can she possibly know this if she's in Huddersfield and I'm in Wakefield!"

She told me loads of other stuff as well – and in particular she mentioned an impending court case that I was very worried about. I'd been issued with a writ because I'd moved away from a hairdressing salon in Leeds city centre and all of my customers had followed me. I was being sued for breach of contract, which was a bit of a joke because I'd

44

never signed a contract in the first place. Even so it was all very worrying. Una said that this court case wasn't anything to worry about and that it would all be resolved in my favour – and lo and behold, within a few weeks, so it was! She also said "you've got a lovely plaque on the wall next to you that you've just brought back from London, and it looks very nice!"

Well, I had just come back from London where I'd been doing some work for a hairdressing magazine, and they had given me this lovely wooden plaque, and I did have it on my wall right next to where I was making the phone call. I thought "yeah, well if this is how it works, I want to do this!"

Anyway, from there I went on to join the spiritualist church and it was almost like coming home. I met other people like myself who could hear spirit voices and realised that I wasn't really going nuts – only that I was just a little bit odd.

The only thing was, I felt that many of the mediums were a little bit vague in some of the things they were saying and I itched for the moment when I could get up on the platform and show other people what I could do. I knew that I could do it, it was just that I needed to be shown how. I got very frustrated when a visiting clairvoyant would say something like "if you don't understand what I'm saying now, just take it with you, my dear..."

When I did finally get out onto the platform it was all very different. It came out like machine gun fire, and half the time I didn't know what I was saying, but I knew I was hitting the target more times than not, and certainly everyone in my audience seemed to enjoy it.

This was where I first met Jane McDonald. I remember seeing her and thinking that she looked like a very nice person. She was a bundle of fun and I really wanted to meet her... Oddly enough it was her Grandmother who introduced us. Jane's Grandma was a lady called Janet Fergussen who was very strong in the church and it was she who first took me up onto the rostrum at Wakefield Spiritualist Church. We did a couple of messages each, just to give me some confidence – and I never looked back from then on.

I served my apprenticeship in the spiritualist churches. To this day spiritualism is the foundation of all my beliefs and it is spiritualism that I am promoting in my evenings of clairvoyance. I'm quite happy giving demonstrations in the churches, but I want to reach new people. I want to get to Joe Public who wouldn't be seen dead in a spiritualist church. I want to prove to them that I can give accurate clairvoyance and pass messages from their loved ones. I want them to see that I'm just a normal bloke and that spiritualism is a very normal, natural thing. I want them to come into the spiritualist church of their own accord, and I want them to see that it isn't all darkened rooms with little old ladies peering into crystal balls. I want people to know that I am proud to be a spiritualist...

I've been asked by quite a few people if I would be interested in training to be a teacher... Well the answer is no, I would not, because I can't teach what I've learned... Whatever I've learned has all happened instinctively and naturally....

I want people to know that I am totally committed to spiritualism because we're like The Halifax Building Society – we offer that little bit extra, and in this case, that little bit extra is a BIG extra. It's proof of survival. I don't like blind faith and in spiritualism more so than in any other religion, we don't have blind faith – we have conclusive PROOF of everlasting life.

Chapter Seven: Terms Of Reference

For more than twenty years I have offered my services as a psychic but I have always been very careful to avoid using the word "clairvoyant" in any of my advertising or publicity material. Many people might ask, "what's the difference?" – and yet there is a very significant difference between the two energies.

First of all, if we take the word clairvoyant, this simply translated from the French, means clear vision, which is something that we all enjoy in our lives. With use and absorption into the English language it has, however, taken on a somewhat different meaning, inferring mediumship and spiritualism.

Putting it very simply, if you are having a sitting with a clairvoyant it is generally assumed that any information given by the medium is coming from a third party in a purely spiritual dimension. This could be a relative or a friend, or even the clairvoyant's own spiritual guide – in essence, anyone who has passed from this world to the next who has some link, no matter how tenuous, with the sitter.

In a *psychic* reading, that third spiritual party is absent and the energy that brings the information through is generated by the reader's mental energy coalescing with the sitter's own spiritual and emotional vibration. The clairvoyant goes with the flow of what ever spiritual energies are present, but the psychic needs to focus and probe to find his answers.

Many psychics blatantly cheat by asking innocent but confirmational questions, such as "do you know what I mean?" or "do you understand?" If they get an affirmative answer, they pursue their lead to a natural conclusion, but if they get a negative response, they simply abort and go on to something else. Even practitioners who do not ask these leading questions will frequently be studying their client's body language and the reaction in their client's eyes to see whether or not they are "hitting" or "missing" – all of which is, of course, both lamentable and deplorable. They do themselves no favours, they mislead their clients, and generally bring the whole subject into ridicule and disrepute.

Take a tip. If you are going to see a psychic, tell them absolutely nothing – give nothing away by word or reaction – and judge them by what *they* tell *you!*

By all means, if you are consulting an astrologer, a date and time of birth is a necessary part of the process; after all, you couldn't expect a mathematician to work out the sum without first providing him with the numbers – which, of course brings us to the ancillary crafts of astrology, palmistry, tarot cards, runes, etc.

The thing to remember about *these* subjects is that they are just crafts. Anyone can learn how to use them without being in any way psychically gifted – but to give credit where it is due, if one was consciously *looking* for ways in which to enhance one's own psychic sensitivity (which is something that we all have somewhere deep down inside ourselves) the study of any of these crafts can frequently be a short cut in opening the doors of inner awareness.

Even so, this is still not clairvoyance in the spiritual definition of the word, and tarot cards and runes are a world away from the talents of Stephen Holbrook and his kind.

And there is, of course, another endemic problem. Time and time again I have met people who have *claimed* to be clairvoyant, when in truth this is simply not the case. They may have some extra sensory perception, some finely tuned intuition, and they may have some genuine psychic ability, which through lack of knowledge they call clairvoyance because that is what they assume it to be. Within this group of people there is a sub-group of folk who would so *like* to be clairvoyant that they deliberately fool themselves (and sadly other people too) into believing that they are indeed gifted in this way. These people are dangerous, not only to themselves but also to others, and should be avoided at all costs.

48

If I say to someone "Hy, my name is James Christie and I'm psychic!" then, if asked to, I believe I can substantiate the claim. So many people I have met have laid claim to being clairvoyant, but when asked to prove this claim, they have crumpled like a house of cards filled with lame excuses. True clairvoyance is a very rare thing indeed, and it is a sobering thought to consider that there are probably less than a hundred people in the whole of the UK who are genuinely clairvoyant, and significantly less than that who are prepared to go out on the road night after night putting themselves to the test by proving it.

These people are usually very ordinary people, with ordinary lives; they have families, hopes and fears (and frequently debts) just like the rest of us. They are not gods and neither are they angels – but through some obscure twist of brain pattern or DNA they are able to communicate with what, to all intents and purposes, is another world. Some people might call that other world Heaven, although Stephen prefers to call it "another dimension of spiritual consciousness" and it is my own belief that the "other world" under discussion is what each and every one of us will expect it to be within the framework of our own belief structure and expectation.

I find it excruciatingly sad that while billions of pounds are squandered every year on bombs and defence budgets not to mention dubious commercial enterprises and national follies, not a penny is provided either by government or church as a body politic to mount some sympathetic but objective research into the phenomenon of clairvoyance and the concept of a spiritual afterlife.

The scientific community scoffs at such concepts when in reality here is the greatest scientific challenge of our time! Where do we go when we die? How is it that a very small number of people can consistently prove that there is an afterlife by opening up a line of communication between the two worlds? Is it that science, state and clergy are afraid of the possible answers, or is it that they are just totally apathetic?

I was having a premeditated discussion with a scientist friend up at York university last week, who rather haughtily pointed out that from a scientific point of view there "is absolutely no proof at all whatsoever of life after death." I countered his opinion by suggesting that although in scientific terms there might not be absolute tangible proof of life after death, from the beginning of recorded time there has been a solid flow of evidence in favour of the concept, and that conversely, from a "purely scientific point of view" there was absolutely no evidence for *no* life after death. He didn't like this argument, wasn't even able to give me a considered response, and ultimately went off in a huff leaving Charlie Muggins to pay for the drinks.

Over the years both Stephen and I have had to deal with a fair amount of scepticism. I actually think that a little scepticism is quite healthy, but inevitably some people take it to extraordinary extremes, denying any evidence that goes against their own pattern of beliefs. It might be okay to say that there are no crocodiles in the river because you haven't actually seen one – but it would be a bit damn silly to say that while you were being eaten by one. And yet, incredible though it might seem, there *are* a few people out there who are like that. In fact I met one quite recently.

Not for the first time the sceptic will claim that Stephen's work is faked and that he is conning his audience...

How then, I asked this one man a couple of weeks ago, can Stephen talk to an absolute stranger on the back row of the stalls and tell them (a) that their name is June, (b) that they lost their father to a heart attack within the previous six months, (c) that the father's name was George, (d) that he was buried on a Wednesday, and (e) that June put a photograph of the family and a St. Christopher medallion in the coffin just before the lid was closed?

50

'Oh that's effing easy, innit,' the sceptic guffawed, 'E's got plants in the audience – a load o'bloody plants!'

Now this is plainly stupid. On average Stephen will deliver more than a dozen messages a night to a dozen different people. He will visit three or four towns a week, frequently many many miles apart. The concept of finding forty or fifty "plants" in any one week is a logical absurdity – and as anyone with a half-open mind would have to admit, it simply could not be done. Thus, to the band of sceptics who say that clairvoyance and communication with the dead is impossible, and therefore by definition, that Stephen is a fraud, I present this challenge… Tell me how he does it – or if you can't do that, present me with a viable, alternative theory that explains his ability to act as a medium between two worlds and bring over the degree of specific evidence that he so consistently brings over, night after night after night!

Chapter Eight: Callum

When, in the late summer of 1998, Hayley Clarke discovered that she was pregnant she was both surprised and delighted. The year before, she'd given birth to her first child, a son called Brad, and now this new pregnancy provided her and her partner Sean with the icing on the cake!

It was a remarkably straight forward pregnancy leading up to what must be one of the easiest confinements in medical history. It was all over in forty five minutes – two gentle pushes and baby Callum popped into the world in the evening of April 24th 1999, weighing in at a healthy six pounds twelve and a half ounces.

Unlike some babies that look like a squashed up version of Winston Churchill, baby Callum was of the new breed – fine elfin features, thick black hair, enormous eyes with lashes that might make a budding starlet go green with envy. In short, the kind of baby that one might look at and muse "well, *he's* been here before, hasn't he!"

Callum passed the usual post-natal health checks with flying colours and the bonding energy between Callum and his parents was both ardent and profound: here was a *good* baby who took his food with little fuss, rarely needed winding and for the better part slept soundly through the night without waking or wanting. Hayley would frequently find herself singing to her newborn son, humbled and at the same time overjoyed by his presence in her life. For his part Callum would follow Hayley around the room with a pair of bright blue eyes that shone with awareness and intelligence. Everything in the Clarke garden was rosy – in fact it was more than rosy – it was absolutely perfect.

The first note of disquiet sounded on Wednesday 26th of May. While playing with the baby and tickling his feet Hayley noticed that the middle toe of Callum's left foot seemed disproportionately longer than the rest of his tiny digits. To say that this caused her any undue alarm would be an exaggeration, but it was something she was *aware* of. It certainly didn't seem to be causing Callum any problems, but it was something she resolved to keep an eye on, never-the-less.

On the following day, Thursday 27th of May, Callum developed a small problem that obviously *did* cause him some distress. Sobbing quietly and waving his hand in the air brought Hayley's attention to the fact that the index finger of his left hand was swollen with some sort of infection. Remembering that she was already uneasy about the elongated toe, she didn't think twice and immediately booked the baby in for an appointment with the doctor.

On Friday 28th May Hayley's GP gave Callum a close inspection and could find nothing intrinsically wrong: the infected finger had already begun to heal itself and because there was no obvious discomfort from the toe, it was left on a "let's wait and see" basis. Reassured that there was nothing too much to worry about, Hayley and her family got on with the business of enjoying the forthcoming weekend.

Tuesday 1st June ended like any normal day. Callum fell asleep in his crib next to Sean and Hayley's bed, and a little while later Brad was settled down for the night in his own bedroom. Hayley and Sean enjoyed an evening meal, watched some TV and went to bed themselves around eleven o'clock. Callum seemed to be sleeping easily enough at that time – but both Hayley and Sean were woken a couple of hour's later around 1.30 AM on Wednesday 2nd June. Callum was restless and uncharacteristically fretful and nothing that the parents could do seemed to ease his distress. In the end, after some considerable time of soothing and cuddling, the baby finally dozed off cradled in his father's arms. Sean gently laid Callum back in his crib, and the couple tried to catch up on the first night of lost sleep their new baby had caused them.

Neither parent slept well.

Sean struggled out of bed and left for work around six o'clock, at which time Hayley, Brad and Callum were sleeping peacefully. But when at 7.45 Hayley climbed out of bed to check on her son she immediately knew that something was dreadfully wrong. The baby's skin colour was ashen grey, every part of his tiny body was pain sensitive to her touch, and most alarming of all, the baby's eyes had rolled up into its head, showing nothing but the whites.

Thus began one of the most intensely distressing and suspenseful three days that any family might fear to experience in their darkest nightmares.

An ambulance was called for and baby Callum was duly admitted to the special care baby unit at Warwick hospital. The day progressed agonisingly slowly as a number of prescribed tests and examinations were undertaken.

Hayley and Sean sat in the waiting room, holding hands in mute disbelief at this sudden turn of events. Various members of the hospital staff would occasionally smile encouragingly and they were never less than supportive, but the suspense of not knowing what was wrong and what the prognosis might be was excruciating in the extreme.

At five o'clock in the afternoon and after nine hours of unendurable tension, the medical team at Warwick Hospital advised Hayley and Sean that Callum was "very poorly" and that he was being immediately transferred to Leicester Royal Infirmary.

Following the ambulance in their car there then followed a high speed drive through the most monstrous thunder storm middle England had seen for many a long year. With rain cascading against the windscreen in deluges and lightening forks stabbing into the landscape all around them, it was a white knuckle ride in more ways than one. Reminiscent of a scene from Gotterdamerung, the word *meningitis* kept flicking through Hayley's mind, and although nobody had used this word in connection with Callum's condition, she could not help wondering whether this terrible twilight storm was in sympathy with the twilight of her baby's life.

Once Callum had been admitted to Leicester Royal Infirmary his parents were allowed to see him, which in itself was a shocking experience. Wired up to a life support machine, his tiny body, so frail and defenceless, seemed to be a pin cushion for a dozen different lines and drips, but on a more positive note the emergency care team told Sean and Hayley that meningitis was low on their list of probabilities.

Knowing that their eldest son was safely being looked after by Sean's sister Siobhan, the couple settled in for an all night vigil at the Leicester Hospital. Hayley's mother and Father, Sandra and Tony, sat with them, but there was little anyone could do other than sit and wait for any kind of news from the medical team.

Through these long hours there was little change in Callum's condition, but at seven o'clock in the morning of Thursday 3rd June baby Callum went into cardiac arrest and a team of seven doctors fought for many tense minutes to save his life. To their credit they were able to pull the little boy back from the brink but the prognosis was grave – so grave, in fact, that Hayley and Sean called a priest and their baby was baptised even as he battled for his life.

At three o'clock that afternoon Callum had a second major heart attack, and for a second time the dedicated team of doctors and nurses at The Leicester Royal Infirmary helped him hang on to a flickering spark of life. This time, however, it took well over an hour to resuscitate him, and there were now serious worries about brain damage having been caused by oxygen starvation.

By now Hayley and Sean had gone for more than thirty hours without sleep – thirty hours of fear and terror with a huge Damoclean sword hovering above their heads. Hayley remembers that they took a walk in the hospital gardens, that they were both in tears, and that Sean prayed aloud that if

God was going to take anyone, let it be him and not his precious new born son!

In truth, both parents were now having to face the fact that the chances of their baby pulling through this ordeal were extremely slim.

At four o'clock that afternoon the blood tests came through from Warwick indicating that Callum had acute septicaemia and (confirming all of Hayley's fears) the rare streptococcal B strain of the meningitis virus.

Callum remained critical but stable throughout Thursday night and there was little that Hayley and Sean could do other than to settle down and spend another exhausting night at their infant's bedside. Neither of them slept very much and Hayley's eyes were constantly drawn to the screen that was measuring Callum's erratic heart beat. Even the most minute change of nuance in rhythm had her leaning forwards with her own heart in her mouth.

On the morning of Friday 4th June, LRI conducted a full brain scan, leading to more interminable hours of dread and suspense. The results of the scan came through at three o'clock in the afternoon indicating that baby Callum was 100% brain dead. They were told that whatever happened this was irreversible, and that it was only a matter of time, to be measured in hours rather than days, before the baby would have another, and this time inevitably fatal, cardiac arrest.

There then followed what was the worst time in their lives. Arguably the worst time imaginable in *any* parent's life.

After much prayer, soul searching and counselling, and following the advice of the doctors, Callum was disconnected from the life support system. At four forty five on the afternoon of June 4th, one day short of being six weeks old, the little boy quietly died.

The Concise Oxford Dictionary gives, as it's meaning of the word "devastation", the following interpretations: *1) to lay waste 2) to cause great destruction 3) to overwhelm with shock or grief 4) to deeply upset.* As with many words currently in vogue, it is a word frequently misused and misapplied. How often do we hear on the news that someone was "devastated" when they lost an inconsequential court case, or when someone has been let down in a job, or when some cheap package deal holiday goes badly wrong? Yes, there are times when it is used correctly, but even then, with common usage the deeper understanding of the meaning of the word is diminished by familiarity.

Therefore if I tell you that Hayley and Sean were devastated by the tragic loss of their six week old son, I present the word in its most literal sense. For a while they *did* feel as though their lives had been destroyed. They *were* deeply upset and they *were* overwhelmed with a profound sense of shock and grief. Amid the dark cavalcade of emotions there were feelings of anger and disbelief – how could this have happened, especially when things had seemed to be going so well – and more importantly, *why* had this had to happen? Was this the will of an all seeing all caring God, and if so what the hell was God playing at – giving life to a beautiful baby and then changing His mind about the whole thing six weeks later no matter what anyone else thought about it? Or, if there was no God and Callum's death was down to random chance in a perverse ungoverned universe, why had such terrible dice been rolled against them and who had rolled those cubes of death?

Hayley and Sean suffered, and if there was one hint of a silver lining amidst this dark cloud of tragedy it came in the form of the support and understanding they received from their family and friends who, deeply affected by Callum's passing over in their own ways, rallied round to provide a cocoon of protection and sympathy.

Indeed, at Callum's funeral, while Hayley managed to get through the day without collapsing into an emotional wreck, other members of the family were constantly near to tears.

One specific incident occurred that demands narration, which concerns Hayley's brother-in-law and sister-in-law, Rob and Barbara.

While still in the chapel of rest, a photograph of Callum, Sean and Brad had been placed in Callum's tiny coffin. Rob also enclosed his silver crucifix, which he lovingly placed around Callum's neck. Unfortunately, unbeknown to anyone, Barbara had gone out and bought a small gold crucifix expressly for this purpose, and now, being pipped to the post as it were, she became very upset indeed.

Sean quietly resolved this the next day by taking Barbara back into the chapel and moving Rob's cross from Callum's neck to his feet, replaced it with the gold cross that Barbara had bought. Thus both relatives were appeased and the coffin was finally sealed containing the family photograph and *two* crucifixes.

Hayley and Sean buried their baby and got on with the task of living their lives: Sean had his work to get back to and they both had Brad to think about and look after. Steadily, and in their different ways, they began to work through the grieving process that comes with bereavement. It didn't happen quickly and it wasn't easy. One thing that Hayley did do was plant a rose tree – a Calluna Rose – in her garden of remembrance.

A number of years earlier, more out of interest than any great desperate need, Hayley had attended a demonstration of clairvoyance given by Doris Collins, and although she had not been expecting a "message" one had actually come through from her late Grandfather which had impressed Hayley enough for her to accept that there might be more than just a little truth in the concept of spiritualism.

But now, in the summer of 1999, things were very different. Her baby had been snatched from her and she was desperate to discover some meaning as to how and why this could have happened. Now she *did* need some proof and reassurance that there was life beyond death, for no matter who she talked to, be it friend, relative or counsellor, no answers seemed to be forthcoming. Try as hard as she might, whatever she did, wherever she went, she carried a cloud of dark misery with her that nothing seemed to be able to alleviate.

When she learned that Stephen Holbrook was to visit Stratford-upon-Avon in November of 1999 she immediately booked tickets. She'd never heard of this particular medium, but that hardly mattered. Any port in a storm and any chance was better than no chance at all.

On the evening of November 14th Hayley and her Mum were among the first to arrive at Stratford's prestigious Falcon Hotel. They took their seats, and sat through the first half of Stephen's demonstration, much impressed by his evidence, and as far as Hayley was concerned, willing his attention over to their part of the room in the hope that there might be something in the ether concerning Callum. When the interval break came without Stephen having so much as even looked their way once, Hayley was quite convinced that she would be returning home empty handed.

However, half way through the second half, the medium's attention did swing over to Hayley's corner of the room, and Hayley takes up the story from there.

'He said he had a connection with someone who'd passed over with brain damage – and then he changed it from brain damage to brain disease – he said that he thought that this might be somebody's son who had passed over some time in the last year, and that this would have been a little boy who was very very young. He wanted to know if anyone could take this information, so I waved my hand and said yes, and he came to me immediately with the number six, and said that he felt this number was very important for some reason, which obviously it was because Callum was just six weeks old when he died. Then he told me he was getting the letter "C" very strongly, which was when I started getting very emotional. I told him that Callum had died when he was only six weeks old, and then Stephen said "well he isn't dead now because he's right here next to me, and he's telling me to tell you that the photograph you put in the coffin is still with him, and he's also saying that there was some trouble about what else went into the coffin. He's also telling me that you planted a tree in the garden, and I think it must have been a rose tree, and that he's grown since he's been on the other side and right now he's as tall as that tree. He's pointing to his left foot and telling me that there was something odd about one of his toes - that it was longer than it should have been and that you were worried about it. He's sending you all his love, but says that he can't hang around to talk now because he wants to be off playing with his mates..."

'Stephen wanted to know if any of this made sense to me and of course it *all* made sense to me, every last little bit of it. The only thing that was a bit confusing was the way Callum talked through Stephen... I mean you'd have thought he was six *years* old, not just six weeks, so obviously something has happened to him since he crossed to the other side, but I don't have any answers for that and I don't think it matters. As far as I'm concerned Stephen Holbrook has given me absolute proof that my son is still alive, even though he may be gone from me down here. He talked about things that nobody but me and my family could know about, and to be so specific about the photograph and the trouble with what went into the coffin, the rose tree in the garden, the business with his toe, the number six and that big letter "C", the brain disease tying in with someone who had passed over while they were still very very young... I mean, how much evidence does a person need?'

Three months after Stephen's demonstration in Stratford-upon-Avon Hayley Clarke kindly consented to meet me at The

Falcon Hotel. It is on the strength of that interview that I have drawn the source material for this chapter, and I take this opportunity to thank her most sincerely for opening her heart to me and telling me the story of Callum from her own unique point of view. Towards the end of what, in many ways, was quite a harrowing morning, I asked her how she felt about things twelve weeks down the road from her experience with Stephen.

She smiled, and the smile was filled with a gentle radiance. 'Stephen changed my life,' she said candidly. 'Oh, I still miss Callum every hour of every day, but since that evening when Stephen spoke to me, the dark cloud that had been hanging over me ever since Callum died, well, it just evaporated. Now I'm able to get on with my life secure in the knowledge that Callum is having a great time somewhere else, and that one day we'll be together again. I don't have all the answers, I don't suppose anyone does, but Stephen Holbrook gave me the strength to tackle life again. That night, after his demonstration, I went home on wings of light and air - I couldn't wait to tell Sean what had happened, and when I did, we both just sat at the kitchen table and cried and cried and cried... But it marked a turning point in my life, and now I can get on with living and looking to the future, knowing that there *is* a future, and not just for me, but for all of us.'

Chapter Nine: Mr Raincoat

Retford is a small town in North Nottinghamshire. Its history can be traced back to before Magna Carta and its latter and present day claim to fame is associated with its excellent three day market. The people of Retford are polite and welcoming without being overly effusive. They know that their town isn't London or York or Oxford or Cambridge, but they are quietly proud of it none-the-less. This pride seems to have seeped into the stonework and Retford presents itself as an honest merchant, modestly confident of its own quality and worth. In short, not the kind of place you would automatically associate with murder and hatred and the desire for the darkest kind of revenge.

Stephen's first demonstration in Retford for Shoestring (which by that time had changed its name to something more conservative) was in the November of 1999. To say that this evening was a success is something of an understatement and therefore when he returned in March 2000 we were in the unfortunate position of having to turn many people away from the doors.

Retford Little Theatre, established for more than seventy five years and run by a dedicated team of local amateurs who present a varied programme of productions over the year, is an absolutely first rate venue which puts many so called professional venues to shame. Jim Wilson and his team crew a very tight ship, and although the theatre is manned by volunteers, any one of them would qualify for a well paid job in London's West End. The only downside is that at capacity RLT can only seat an audience of 160, and almost as many as that were disappointed on the night of March 30th.

Prior to the demonstration both Stephen and I were elated at the strong turn out, but oddly enough it wasn't a particularly good night for the medium and the first half of the evening saw him struggling to bring over clear concise messages.

When he collapsed into the dressing room for the interval and greedily guzzled the pint of Coca-Cola I usually had standing by, he was bathed in a lather of perspiration and anxiety.

'What's the problem?' I asked, trying to bring him down from his state of agitation.

'James, I honestly don't know – it's as though there's something out there deliberately blocking me, and no matter what I do I can't seem to get through it. I've never known anything quite like this before. I mean, you always get the odd problem when you're faced with a total sceptic, but this isn't anything like that. It's almost as though there's someone out there in the audience who is *deliberately* willing me to keep my mouth shut and whoever it is, they've got a lot of power around them – a lot of very negative and hostile power.'

I thought for a moment, applying some skill and knowledge that were not generally in Stephen's own armoury. 'Can you identify where it's coming from in relationship to the audience?' I asked.

'I hadn't thought about that,' he wiped his face with a towel, 'but now when I *do* think about it, maybe somewhere in the middle of the room? About half way back?'

'Okay, when you go back on stage, take your time. Try focusing on where the bad vibes are coming from, and as soon as you've got a fix, go for the jugular vein. See what you can pick up and deal with it – because if you don't you're going to need more than a pint of Coke by the end of the night.'

'All right – I don't know if it will work, but I'll give it a try...'

Stephen *did* give it a try, and it worked out very well. Rather too well, in fact, and I lost the better part of a night's sleep on the strength of it.

When Stephen walked on stage for the second half of the evening I took up a position by the main entrance to the auditorium, which gave me a clear view both of the stage and the audience.

Hand on my heart, I don't think that he meant to be dramatic about it, but his opening to act two was nothing less than theatrical.

Rather than bouncing on in his usual way, he walked very slowly to the centre of the stage, head lowered in concentration, left arm wracked in its familiar rictus. As the hubbub of conversation died he slowly raised his head and deliberately quartered every part of the auditorium. Finally his eyes came to rest, focused towards the middle of the room and when he spoke it was only after a number of *very* long seconds.

'I want to come to someone in the middle of the sixth or seventh row who actually *doesn't* want a reading from me tonight – which is a bit unusual because by this time in the evening most members of the audience are reasonably tuned in to what I'm trying to do and are hoping that I *will* come to them with a message. This person is carrying a lot of pain and distress with them – and I sense that they are planning to do something quite terrible. Well, I've got that person's Mother talking in my head, and she's saying that although there wasn't much love lost between mother and son when she was alive down here, she really did her best, even though she knows it wasn't always good enough. More importantly she's telling me that she loves you very much and that she really does hope and pray that you won't go ahead with what you're planning to do because it won't help matters at all, in fact, it will only make them worse. She says she's aware of how you feel, she knows all about the anger and the despair, and she knows what you bought last Wednesday in Nottingham and she's telling me that you mustn't use it. Either throw it in the river or take it back to the shop and ask for a refund…. I could say a lot more, but I think I've said enough to get the

64

message over, so I'll leave this with you Sir, and hope that you take this message seriously…'

At this point, a stocky nondescript man in a gabardine raincoat gets up from his seat, walks down the aisle in full view of both Stephen and the audience, brushes past me with a stonelike expression on his face, and makes his exit from the theatre.

This is a very curious situation because at no time has Stephen taken the normal confirmational verbal link with any one – it has been a very one way communication. Furthermore it is extremely unusual for anyone to walk out half way through one of Stephen's demonstrations. And yet, almost with the slamming of the door which heralds the stocky man's departure, the atmosphere in Retford Little Theatre palpably changes, becoming lighter and brighter in the space of just a few heart beats.

It is obvious that Stephen feels this change, for as he moves into the second half of the evening proper, a mood of hilarity and laughter begins to prevail, precipitated in no small part with his next link.

'I've got someone here called Richard,' he explains. 'Can anyone take a Richard?'

Ominous silence, but Stephen is quite insistent. 'Richard is definitely a name that links with *someone* here tonight – he would have passed over in the last couple of years, quite suddenly, and as a result of an accident rather than an illness. Please, can anyone take the name Richard?'

What happens next is not apocryphal, and is made even more effective by the appearance of the young woman who starts waving her hand in the air, just a few feet away from where I am standing. She's wearing a leather skirt, has got enormous breasts, bouffanted blond hair and bright red lips.

She comes to her feet… 'I don't know a Richard.' She calls out, 'but I can take a Dick!'

The audience collapses with a roar of laughter as the poor girl looks puzzled and bemused, obviously not aware of how her words have been interpreted. Then the penny drops and she too collapses into a fit of giggles. She gets her message, but no one, not even she, is paying too much attention to it.

There *is* the apocryphal story, told by Doris Collins about Doris Stokes, when in similar circumstances someone claimed to be able to "take a Willie" with much the same reaction as occurred at Retford Little Theatre, and there is an even more bizarre tale of the clairvoyant who had a link with someone from the world of circus and wanted to know if anyone in the audience could "take an elephant" - but the Richard/Dick link seems to be a most appropriate association for our present times, and although Stephen might squirm with embarrassment, it has relevance to the working life of a modern medium and I see no reason to act as censor.

More, however, was yet to come.

'I have a voice directing me to a lady three rows back, five seats in from the end... Yes, you madam, the lady in the cream jacket. I've got a gentleman here called Sam. He says he's your husband and...'

'Tell 'im to go back,' the woman yells from the stalls emphatically. 'I couldn't stick 'im!'

More laughter and merriment from the crowd who is loving every minute of what has now become a very light-hearted and entertaining evening.

Stephen came through with another half dozen strong messages and unlike the first half of the show, the second half ended on something of an all time high.

Later, I spoke to Stephen about the first message of the second half and of the man who had left the auditorium.

'Oddly, I don't remember too much about it, and I didn't realise that I was actually talking to that particular chap until he got up and left the room... I just had this lady standing on the stage next to me and putting the words into my mouth...

But what a difference after he'd left! I just hope he's all right, wherever he is.'

'Do you know what the message meant?' I asked. 'From the audience's point of view it all sounded a bit dramatic and mysterious.'

Stephen shook his head. 'Sorry James, I haven't a clue!' And, of course, neither had I. Not then. But I was to find out what it was all about just a little later.

Stephen had already left and I was sorting out the last bit of business with the theatre management before hitting the road myself, when the foyer doors swung open and in strode our stocky friend in the gabardine raincoat. With thunder clouds threatening imminent detonation hovering over his head he marched over to where I was stuffing the last few unused flyers into my battered briefcase and demanded to see Mr Holbrook.

I explained that Stephen had gone for the night but Mr Raincoat was adamant. 'No, I'm sorry, you don't understand. I've simply *got* to talk to him. Give me his address and his phone number and wherever he's gone I'll get in my car and catch him up!'

'I'm afraid I can't do that, Sir. There's no way I'm going to give you Stephen's address or his phone number. I'm not authorised to do so. What I *can* do is take *your* number and ask Stephen to give you a call in the morning...'

'No that won't do at all!' He grabbed at my arm. 'I've got to talk to your man tonight!'

Even though there was no small degree of desperation in his voice I neither liked his tone nor his attitude. There was no smell of alcohol on his breath and his eyes, although angry in expression, were clear from the unfocused haze that might suggest some form of substance abuse. Even so, I was tired and this gentleman was seriously rubbing me up the wrong way.

'It isn't going to happen,' I said quietly but firmly, prising his fingers from my arm.

He looked at me blankly for a second, and then the expression in his eyes changed. In the space of one short moment all the hostility departed to be replaced with an expression of unutterable despair. Without warning he suddenly turned away from me and burst into uncontrollable sobs.

Now there have been a couple of times in my life when I have had my back to the wall and exactly the same thing has happened to me. It was, therefore, very difficult for me to turn away from this fellow without trying to offer some degree of help. I desperately wished that I could just direct him into Stephen's arms and let him sort it out – but by then Stephen was half way up the motorway heading back to his home and family, and in any case, this was the kind of thing that the promoter was *supposed* to deal with.

I steered Mr Raincoat out of the theatre and into the car park. It was raining a damp March drizzle, and even though the neon lights of Retford offered some reflected cheer, it was still a pretty miserable place to be. Initially I wasn't sure what to do, so did nothing other than rest a hand lightly on Mr Raincoat's shoulder and let him get the tears out of his system.

After a few minutes, he pulled away, wiping his eyes with a less than clean handkerchief and gasping in huge lungfuls of cool night air. 'Okay – be all right now – thanks a lot.'

'Look,' I said, 'I really can't give you Stephen's number, but I can take yours and I *will* get him to call you in the morning… Or if you think I might be able to help you in some way, well look, there's a pub just over the road, and quite frankly you look as though you could do with a drink…'

Cutting a long story short we went over to the pub, got our drinks and found a quiet corner – which wasn't difficult as the bar was virtually empty. Frankly, it was a rather poor place, devoid of atmosphere, but at least the bright lights allowed me to examine my companion's face in some detail. He was in his early forties with regular features and wearing quite expensive clothes. Now that all the anger had gone from his face it was easy to see that the guy was in some extreme emotional distress. The best thing to do in any counselling session is to get your subject to open up and talk about what's bothering them, but before he was prepared to do that Mr Raincoat (and for reasons which will become obvious in a moment or so, I'm going to carry on calling him that) needed some questions answered.

'How was he able to *do* that?' he marvelled. 'I mean, to be able to pick me out from all those people, to know how I was feeling, and to know about my Mother and how we felt about each other?' He took a liberal swig of his drink, and then eyed me darkly. 'And how did he know what I bought in Nottingham last week?'

'He didn't,' I explained patiently. 'The message that he got from your Mother simply said that you *had* bought something that you should either take back or throw in the river. She didn't tell Stephen what it was…'

There then followed a very potted presentation on the subject of mediumship and clairvoyance; for the better part he seemed to listen to most of it, but there were times when his attention wandered off. In the end I left it with him to direct the next turn of the conversation.

'Do *you* know what it was?' he asked.

'Sorry,' I said. 'I'm missing you. What *what* was?'

'What I bought in Nottingham last week.'

'No, I have no idea.'

'Do you want to see it?' he asked – and now there was a crafty note in his voice that alerted me to the fact that although sober and now relatively calm, this guy had some very serious problems somewhere in his psyche.

'Yes sure,' I answered, 'if you've got it with you and you want me to see it.'

69

Glancing around to make sure no one was looking, he furtively unfastened his coat and lifted the edge of the garment so I could see what was beneath it.

To say that my blood ran cold was an understatement.

He was wearing a dark blue sweater and dark blue denim jeans and a wide leather belt that had nothing to do with keeping his trousers up!

Tucked into the belt was a very large automatic pistol. It gleamed dully in a dark shade of gun metal blue and it was obviously quite new. Mr Raincoat reached inside his coat and stroked the butt affectionately. It looked very mean and deadly, and although it could have been a replica, I was fairly sure that it was the real thing.

'Used to be in the SAS,' he said conversationally, 'and we used these babies quite often. Came in very handy during the Falkland War and the Gulf War I might tell you! Of course, it wasn't standard army issue but most of the lads carried one in their kit for emergency close up work... If you're interested, it's a Browning 9mm, takes fifteen rounds with one up the spout. Don't usually like American stuff, but this is a real beauty! Of course, you can't buy guns like this over the counter any more, not since Dunblane, but it's not as difficult as you might think, providing you know the right people.'

'Fascinating,' I murmured, wondering if I could get to the door and find a phone before he had time to get the evil looking weapon out of his belt, 'but the question is, what the hell is it doing here?'

Mr Raincoat's story is sad but in some respects not entirely uncommon. Take a professional army man discharged after twenty years service on medical grounds who finds it increasingly difficult to come to terms with civilian life and even more difficult to find a job worthy of his talents. See how this erodes the sanctity of a marriage that was never a truly perfect relationship from day one. Accept the inevitability of a wife who becomes so depressed by the daily rounds of arguments and moods of violent dissatisfaction that she seeks solace elsewhere and enters into an extra-marital relationship with a sympathetic colleague at her place of work – this culminating in her demand for a divorce from the husband who has driven her to these extreme measures.

Most husbands would be angry and upset by this turn of events especially if they loved their wives... Most husbands might try to make their wives change their minds, but once it becomes apparent that the wife is not going to change her mind, most husbands might begin to accept the inevitability of separation and divorce. Unfortunately Mr Raincoat doesn't fall into the category of "most husbands" and once he realised that his wife and her new lover intended to try and build a new life for themselves, he resolved to do something about it.

Mrs Raincoat had moved out of the marital home a fortnight previously and was now living with her new partner with divorce papers in the pipeline. Mr Raincoat made up his mind that there was not going to be a divorce, and if he could not prevent it by legal means he would prevent it by highly *illegal* means. He had bought the gun with the clear intention of killing both his wife and her lover, and after that, depending how he felt about things, he would probably kill himself also.

This idea was not an impulsive thing. He had been mulling it over and planning it for days. He was well aware of the fact that he was irrational although he did not believe himself to be insane. Indeed, in the interim period he had sought help from his local GP, the parish priest, social services and The Samaritans – all to no avail. On the night of March 30th 2000 he had been on his way to his wife's new home with the loaded pistol, and his route had taken him past the front of Retford Little Theatre just as Stephen's demonstration was about to begin. On impulse he had bought a ticket and had gone inside – perhaps in one last desperate attempt to get some help from somewhere, or possibly, because he knew he was early for his appointment with death and he just wanted to get out of the rain for a while.

There are two postscripts to this story. One, without going into any of the details, is that Mr Raincoat did *not* keep his appointment with death, and after a lot of counselling and many conversations over several weeks, he finally did begin to receive some much needed help from the appropriate medical and psychiatric services. I'd like to think that I might have played a small part in this for it was I who stood by his side in the early hours of an April morning when he finally plucked up the courage to hand the gun over to the officer in charge of his local police station.

Two, some months after the events related, Mr Raincoat joined his own Spiritualist Church, and has on at least three occasions been part of Stephen's audience whenever Stephen has been demonstrating in the North Notts neck of the woods. He is still having problems dealing with the difficult relationship with his Mother and he is still having enormous difficulties coming to terms with the loss of his wife – 'Christ James, I honestly wish she was dead! That would be easier to deal with than knowing that she's alive and happy with someone else!' – but at least the murderous and suicidal tendencies have passed, and slowly but ever so surely Mr Raincoat is on the mend.

In my own mind, I am absolutely convinced that had Mr Raincoat not been drawn into Retford Little Theatre and had he not received the message that he received from Stephen Holbrook, then there would have been a double murder and a suicide before midnight! I am also reasonably convinced that it must have been some form of spiritual intercession that directly drew Mr Raincoat into Stephen's presence.

Chapter Ten: Questions And Answers

I asked Stephen how he felt when he was actually in the process of giving clairvoyance. He tells me that he is totally tuned in to the spiritual vibrations that fluctuate around him, but is completely cut off from the outside world.

'A bomb could go off in the street and I wouldn't hear it! Sometimes a mobile phone will start ringing during a demonstration, and although this can be a nuisance from the audience's point of view, it doesn't really bother me. As for what giving clairvoyance actually feels like…? Well, there's this wave of energy gushing and rushing through the whole of my body which is totally exhilarating. It's almost as though I've been taken over by the energy of each spiritual link and with each new link there's a new burst of energy. The energy is different depending on who comes through and who I'm linking with, and this usually depends on what condition the person was in when they passed over. If someone has died in a sudden accident I will feel traumatised, but if they've passed over as a result of a long illness, then usually I find myself feeling very calm and at peace. One of the hardest things to do is to communicate with children because they're all so full of excitement and like any kid, they don't always know how to say what they want to say.

'One of the most difficult things, of course, is to link the message I'm getting to the recipient in the audience. Some people are very shy and nervous and either can't or won't talk to me – which is dreadful because then the message and the link get lost. Then there are some people who didn't realise that there was a message coming through for them until it's too late. If I could say "Hello I've got Jack here who wants to talk to Jill," it would be much easier, but for whatever reason, spirit seldom works quite like that. Sometimes I *do* get a name, but names can be funny things, can't they? I'll say to someone, like that fellow in Ilkley, that I've got a link with

Dorothy, but if she wasn't generally known as Dorothy but as Dotty, people can sit there puzzling who I'm talking about.

'But as soon as I can hear the voice of the recipient, this opens up the airwaves and everything starts gelling together and I know instinctively that I've captured some true evidence of life after death.

'Whenever I'm giving a public demonstration there is usually a clamour of activity from spirits who want to make contact with their loved ones in the audience – a bit like a dozen people milling round the only public phone box in town each with an urgent call to make. I have to sift one message from the other, but it can be hard, what with everyone talking at once. This is why the voice from the audience is so important. It's the only thing that makes the connection.'

Stephen raises a couple of issues here that are worthy of further discussion, not least of which is this business about names.

In my Houdini period (that time when I was looking for evidence of an afterlife, not finding it, and exposing frauds wherever I found them) I would frequently think "if this medium has got so-and-so on the stage with them and they're trying to make a connection with someone who has green fingers and loves gardening, why, for heaven's sake, can't they just name a name?"

To my way of thinking it was and still is a completely logical question – and I suppose this is one reason why I am so impressed by Stephen because despite his earlier words he frequently *does* name names, and if not at the beginning of the link then certainly at some time during the message.

I tackled Stephen about this very early in our association and in response he conducted a most curious experiment to make his point. I have to say that this is an experiment that I have subsequently conducted three or four dozen times myself, and amazingly the results are invariably the same.

What Stephen did was this.

He asked for two volunteers from the audience to come forward, the only criteria being that these two people should know each other very well. Two young ladies came to the front of the room whereupon Stephen stood them back to back, placing himself between his two subjects. He then asked lady number one to tell him something about herself that he could pass on to lady number two that would prove to lady number two that it was genuinely a message from lady number one.

After lots of giggles and no small amount of umming and ahhing lady number one said that she liked men with nice bums.

Stephen then reversed the procedure and asked lady number two to tell him something about herself that he could pass on to lady number one that would prove that it was a message from lady number two.

Lady number two said that she hated Chinese food and that she'd been to Mallorca for her summer holiday.

This procedure went backwards and forwards between the two girls for the better part of ten minutes with comments like...

'I've got a birth mark on my thigh!'

'I'm in love with Mel Gibson!'

'I want to win a million pounds on the lottery!'

'I've just bought a new car!'

Long before the end of the experiment these two girls were really struggling to come up with anything at all – the umms became longer and the ers and ahhs significantly more frequent. And yet here is the truly amazing thing. Remembering Stephen's initial brief *at no time did either girl give Stephen her name!*

It would have been so easy, wouldn't it, for lady number one to say "Tell her this is Molly" or for lady number two to say "Tell her it's me, Fiona"? And yet it simply didn't happen. Furthermore, in my later trials with this experiment, it seldom happened then.

I accept that this proves nothing, but it is an interesting state of affairs, and I urge you to conduct your own experiment and see what results *you* come up with.

There is another aspect appertaining to names that might be relevant here – and this is *my* theory based on my own research and does not necessarily coincide with Stephen's own views.

Like Stephen I believe that the spirit survives death. Also like Stephen I believe that the spirit retains its personality and more importantly its *identity* after death.

Unlike Stephen, however, I believe in reincarnation and I have no difficulty at all whatsoever in accepting the concept of each of us living many different lives. Those lives may have been lived at hugely disparate times across the aeons of history and will inevitably have given us experience of different cultures and different levels of awareness.

If in this life I am James Christie from York, then people from this life will know me as James Christie, but if in my last life I was Jaime Ortega from Spain or in the life before that I was Heinrich Beerswiller from Munich people from those lives will know me either as Jaime or Heinrich.

When I move from this world into the world of spirit, my spirit will remain the quintessential me with all of my personality traits and idiosyncrasies of character, but if I am trying to convey a message to the earth plane what name shall I use? If as a spirit I am not sure of a name, but I *am* sure of my spiritual identity, is it not logical that I should try to communicate from the point of identity rather than the point of a transient name? If I was trying to get a message through to my wife I could, through someone like Stephen, say "tell her it's her husband and if she wants some proof mention the black hat, the limp and the horn-rimmed glasses," and without any shadow of doubt my wife would recognise my presence on the basis of that description.

And one last point. People don't always like the names they are born with or the names they are called over the years of a life. Given a new life what more natural thing to do but choose a new name for one's spiritual self or to revert to what is a purely spiritual or Angelic name – the name that God gave us rather than the one bestowed upon us by our parents?

When I talked to Stephen about reincarnation he sounded somewhat dubious. 'I can see the purpose behind learning from our mistakes and progressing on a spiritual level, but doesn't it make a mockery of being able to contact Mum or Dad once they've passed over?'

My own feelings are that there is not a conflict of interests here, but this is not a book about what I think and it is certainly not a book about reincarnation – although when we were discussing the subject, Stephen did delight me with the following anecdote.

After a particular demonstration a lady approached Stephen to thank him for bringing a message over from her late husband. 'I was *so* pleased to hear from him,' she said. 'The evidence was overwhelming, and quite frankly, I'm just so relieved!'

'Relieved?' Stephen echoed.

'Oh yes, because some friends of mine who know about these things told me that by now my husband could have already been reincarnated, and that he might even have been reincarnated as a sheep! If you look out of my back kitchen window there's a farmers field full of sheep, and I couldn't help wondering if poor Cedric was out there. One of the sheep came right up to the garden fence and I thought "Oh dear, what if that's my Cedric?"'

Some friends! – And if the lady is reading this let me put her mind at rest. If we are reincarnated at all, we come back as more highly evolved beings and most definitely not as sheep!

For those of you who like statistics, here's a beauty. Did you know that in 1998 alone there were more than three thousand books published in the USA on the subject of Angels? When I asked Stephen about Angels he shook his head somewhat sadly and said that he had no conclusions one way or the other. Inevitably this led me to question him on his vision of heaven, and very refreshingly, I thought, he said that he didn't have one.

'James, I only know what I know. Spirit people who have passed over from this life talk to me and give me messages of encouragement to pass on to their loved ones. I don't know where they are talking to me from, so all I can call it is another plane of spiritual existence. Obviously our spirits go *somewhere* but I have never had any indication of what or where that somewhere is. The communication I have with the spirit world is virtually one way. *They* talk to *me* and I pass on what they tell me. Sure, I try talking to them too, but I've never been in a position where I've been able to interrogate a spirit – and I have to say that to me this isn't all that important. That we survive death is important, that in the afterlife all our wounds are healed, all our fears are calmed – these are the really important things.'

I describe Stephen's attitude as "refreshing" because I have read books by and about other less gifted mediums who seem to have a detailed answer for everything. At best, any kind of answer to the kind of questions I put to Stephen can only be conjecture and theory, or if you will, one person's subjective opinion based on their first hand (and frequently second and third hand!) experiences – and at worst it is wishful thinking and an over active imagination. And yet these "opinions" are often presented as hard incontrovertible facts which do not stand up to the test of objective cross examination because, put simply, until someone actually comes back from the world of spirit and tells us exactly what it is like in the next world, your guess is as good as mine. There are scores of visions, dozens of theories, hundreds of opinions, and a lot of people have got very very rich by writing a lot of very misleading books on just about every aspect of the subject imaginable. For Stephen to say "I don't know" might be a bit annoying to me the writer, and it might be a bit frustrating to you the reader, but we must both applaud the man's total candour and absolute honesty.

Stephen – on Stephen and Mediumship

I know that when I stand in front of an audience, I do not stand alone. I know that my guides and inspirers are with me, I know that they are there to help, and I know they will never let me down.

Some people tend to think that I know everything, but I promise you that this isn't true. I do not! I only know what I hear... Some people get worried and they clam up, because they think I'm going to air all their dirty washing in public, but it doesn't work like that. In fact most of the time I don't know anything about what I'm saying. I know what I'm saying, but not what it's all about. It's like listening to a telephone conversation when you pick up a party line: you can hear what's being said, you could translate it and pass it on, but half the time you wouldn't have a clue about what the other people were talking about...

Some people want to put you on a pedestal, and I hate this, I really do... What I've got is a natural gift, and what I do is act as a channel for the spirit world. If you want to praise and thank anyone, praise and thank the spirits, not me. I want the spirits to take the credit, because at the end of the day all I am is a telephone operator...

Sometimes I get very embarrassed... I'll come to the phone or meet someone in the street and they'll say "ooh it's you!" and I think well of course it's bloodywell me! I'm just a normal bloke, so what did you expect? I might have long blond hair and a bit of a funny nose, but I don't go round wearing white robes or working miracles.

This is something I really want to get across in this book. I want people to know that I'm doing this book not for any kind of personal recognition but for the benefit of people who want to know a bit more about spiritualism, how natural it is, and how you don't have to be gifted or clever or intelligent to become a part of it... And I know that this is true, because I'm none of those things myself!

80

I am very sensitive and until I came to terms with my gift my life was very black and white. Now it's in colour... Like watching a black and white TV for years then suddenly getting a widescreen colour set, or listening to a radio cassette on mono and then getting DVD through a bank of matched speakers...

My own life has become so much more precious to me since I've discovered my gift because I know I can help other people... More than just help... I don't want to sound cocky or arrogant, but I feel that I can give other people some sort of inner strength to deal with their own lives while they are down here. No, I can't live their lives for them and nor would I want to, but I can sometimes act as intermediary between them and their loved ones who have moved over in to spirit, I can assure them they are still loved and cherished, I can promise them that all pain and disease is removed once they make the transition from this world to the next, and I can offer hard factual evidence for life after death.

For the better part, I have loved being a hairdresser. If nothing else it has given me a good grounding in the art of communication. Anyone who has been a hairdresser for more than ten years is better than any psychiatrist! I enjoy the job very much – you have to have very close contact with the client and you have to build a rapport with them. This communications training has helped me enormously with my mediumship – the art of listening to what is being said without trying to change it.

If a message comes through which is very obscure and remote I've still got to say it like it is because although it may mean nothing to me you can bet your life it means something to the person I'm trying to make the link with. If someone in spirit says "tell them about the tray of tomatoes" that's what I've got to pass on because that is what will be important. That is the one thing that will mean something important, however stupid it might seem. It could be "tell her about the flowers" or "tell her about the shed roof" or even "tell her about the glass she broke in the sink this morning". They're all little things but they provide the nitty gritty truth of hard evidence and it is this kind of evidence that I take pride in because it proves the link is real. It's so easy to say "I've got your Mum here" or your son or your Dad, but what I say is, if that's the case, go on and prove it. Give them some firm identification such as "they watched you this afternoon when you were getting rid of that big cobweb in your bedroom" because this is not the sort of thing you would do every day, is it, and if you did get rid of a big cobweb, then there's some proof!

People ask me if I tell the future, and I don't unless I've got absolute proof of ID and the spirit is giving me the information to pass on. If I've got someone on stage with me who tells me his name is Robert and that he died of a heart attack in November 1998 and the link is taken by someone in the audience, then I don't mind passing on anything that Robert might tell me... If he says there is going to be a reunion in the spring and that you're going to see your long lost daughter again, I'm happy to believe him and I'm happy to pass that information on. But I'm not a fortune teller and I don't see the future unless the spirit world gives me that information. I'm a medium and I communicate with the dead – not that they're really dead anyway – and I see myself in ten or twenty years doing exactly the same as I'm doing now, only, God willing, doing it better. I'll never change. I'll always want to be part of the crowd. I don't want to be shoved in a back room like some entertainer waiting to go on and do his turn.

Spiritualism, like my own mediumship, is a very natural thing. We cannot see the fresh air but it touches our faces every day, and we need it to live and exist. Whenever I go out there in front of an audience I always feel nervous – I *never feel totally confident, and I never take my gift for granted. The moment I lose this respect for spirit, I'm likely to come unstuck. At the end of the evening I'll always take ten or fifteen minutes to say thank you to the spirits for helping me in the demonstration...*

As I've said before, my guides act as monitors, and I've got so many different guides who work with me from all different walks of life, from different times and eras, and each has its own specialist subject. Should I get a message from someone who has committed suicide then it's always Warren who will bring the person through. Warren killed himself in a police cell and he's been working with me now for five or six years. He always makes other suicides feel welcome on the platform. Children come through little Christopher, and that's how it goes. One minute you can be talking to a little old lady who found her eighty five year old husband dead in bed next to her, and the next minute you're talking to a young woman who lost a baby when the baby was still only a few months old, then, hey presto, you're back to talking to someone who took their own life in a fit of grief and despair. Obviously just one guide could not monitor all this successfully. A ninety year old lady and a twenty year old punk don't have too much in common, so different guides will serve these different characters and personalities.

I have so many different guides and inspirers working with me on so many different levels and I think this is what amplifies things and makes it so different for me. I can't understand how some mediums lay claim to only having one guide because I've always had so many and sometimes it's like a bloody playground up there on the platform...

Chapter Eleven: In Search Of Archie May

A little while ago I was invited to lunch by a well known clairvoyant lady from London who, over the years, has made quite a name for herself in the national media. This lady, whom I shall refer to as Madam Margaret, had heard that I was writing this book about Stephen Holbrook and wanted to explore the possibility of me writing a similar book about herself. As I was in London for a couple of days anyway, I thought it would do no harm to meet her, and so after I'd finished my business in Covent Garden I grabbed a tube and made the journey down to Wimbledon.

I was met at the door by an apparition in swathes of Barbara Cartland pink who introduced herself as Madam Margaret and who then ushered me through a mausoleum of modern antiques interspersed with New Age artefacts. I was led into a substantial conservatory at the back of the house, poured an enormous glass of Chablis, and then lectured for an hour about how clever and wonderfully spiritual my hostess was. I regret to say that I was bored out of my tree after five minutes, and after ten I was looking for ways to bring the interview to an early end and make my escape.

Sadly this was not to happen and I realised the only way I was going to get back into Central London that night was to go through the motions of conducting the interview.

Thus I allowed Madam Margaret to take me through to the dining room and we sat at a table that was laid not for two but three people. An old fashioned maid dressed in traditional black and white served three bowls of cucumber soup, three plates of smoked salmon sandwiches, and three dishes of sherry trifle. To say that I was bemused by the bizarre situation is the understatement of this chapter and inevitably I had to ask whom the third place had been set for – although even before I asked I had a sneaky idea of what the answer might be.

'Oh my dear, it's for Red Feather, of course!'

'Red Feather?'

'Yes! Red Feather is my Spirit Guide and I always set a place for him at table – or if I'm going to the theatre, or if I'm flying anywhere I *always* book an extra seat for Red Feather!'

In my opinion this is eccentricity in the extreme, but Madam Margaret is by no means unique in claiming spiritual guidance from Native American Indians. At the risk of sounding cynical, I think I must have met them all over the years – White Feather, White Cloud, White Buffalo, Red Feather, Green Feather, Blue Feather, Sitting Bull, Cochise, Geronimo – you name 'em and *someone* will claim them as being their guide!

Then, of course, there are the ubiquitous Chinamen, Monks, Mandarins, Taipans and Taiwanese, not to mention Tibetans, Priests and Priestesses from Egypt and Atlantis... The list is predictably endless, overtaxing the imagination and stretching credulity to breaking point. What is even more worrying is the clairvoyant's enthusiastic willingness to accept the presence of these "guides" without a single shred of hard evidence that they ever existed.

If there are such people as spirit guides (and let me go on record as saying that despite the last couple of paragraphs I do most firmly believe that there are) then why are they not ordinary people – Great Aunt Elizabeth from Chipping Norton or Nellie Throggitt, the fishmonger's wife from Whitby?

Although I am not a medium I do work with psychic forces and when I am in the process of giving a reading I will frequently get some help from spirit: either my Grandmother or Ossie Rae, occasionally another friend who passed over recently, will make their presence felt in my mind and assist me through a difficult part of the consultation. This usually happens when I'm very tired or have no natural empathy with my client, and it happens quietly, unbidden and without drama. I will see my Grandmother sitting on her favourite bench against a Yorkshire stone wall, surrounded by wallflowers – "Tell her about her eyes" she might say – or I'll get a flash image of Ossie wearing a striped tea shirt sitting in his caravan "If he doesn't change his ways this silly sod's going to have a heart attack" he might chuckle – but there are no Chinese Mandarins or Indian Chiefs, no rocking tables, floating trumpets, or sudden drops of temperature. It's a head thing, purely in my mind, no flashing lights, no melodrama. While I would not regard either my Grandmother or Ossie Rae as "ordinary" in the parochial sense of the word, neither are they foreign exotics. As personalities they are relevant to my own time, space and experience, and as such, this makes a lot of sound common sense to me.

I ran these thoughts past Stephen and he came up with some ideas that have had a degree impact on my own somewhat jaded and rather cynical opinions.

He asked me to remember that while the North American Indians were not a sophisticated people, they were a remarkably *spiritual* people who were extremely close both to their deities and to nature – so close, in fact, that they regarded the divide between life and death to be a very fine line indeed, and one in which both man *and* spirit could cross quite freely at will. Their culture was old and more importantly, uncontaminated until the coming of the white man. With the advent of the white invasion a whole culture and belief system was decimated within a couple of hundred years, which opens the doors to a couple of interesting theories.

One, what if a Higher Spiritual Authority deliberately sacrificed the North American Indians for the express purpose of using them as a spiritual guidance system for a developing civilisation that was to be severely flawed by its fundamental *lack* of spiritualism? The North American Indian may have been spiritual and close to nature, but for countless generations he had been static in the physical chain of evolution. For more than a century he has been paralysed by

86

subjugation and tradition, held captive in the concentration camps called reservations, and it is only in the last generation as increasingly he has absorbed the ideas of a new culture, than he has begun to claim his place, reformed and redefined, within what could be described as the modern world order.

This is not Caucasian arrogance and no one pretends that the North American Indian is getting a fair deal in the present socio-economic structure of the USA, but over the last two decades things have begun to change for the better. Who is to say that a hundred years from now the North American Indian, having absorbed new strains of knowledge and after having undergone a necessary metamorphosis, might not re-emerge as the dominant species of Homo Sapiens on that continent?

The second theory is more simple and less controversial. To all intents and purposes the white man wiped out the red man. Dismiss from your mind the Hollywood version of the North American Indian and see him more clearly as the introspective and insular peace loving soul who fought by his own ethical standards but only to protect his land from invasion and erosion. Consider it a possibility that on a spiritual level he was far more advanced than we could ever hope to be, and because of this, armed not with the tomahawk but with a genuine desire to make us more like him, he now works with forgiveness through the veils of karma and time to redress an imbalance – albeit not one of his own making.

Addressing the Chinese/Tibetan/Eastern energy of spirit guides, one must not forget they too were (and are) remarkably more spiritually orientated than ourselves: this is the very nature of Buddhism, Shinto, Zen, etc., and these belief structures offer a significantly deeper philosophical structure than Christianity, Judaism or even Islam. Is it not logical then that more spiritually advanced energies from the Eastern hemispheres of this planet should be in a powerful position to offer us some insight and guidance? As for Egyptians, Sumerians, Atlanteans (if indeed they ever existed) then again, why not? These older civilisations were highly advanced in art and science and even technology while the rest of the world wandered around in animal skins, living in caves and grunting in neo-Neanderthal monosyllables!

By this time Stephen was revved up and raring to go, so it seemed an opportune moment for me to ask him about his own spirit guide – hoping against hope, despite all that he'd already said, that he wasn't going to introduce me to White Bird or Brown Owl. I need not have worried for quite typically it would seem that Stephen's spirit guide is someone significantly more down to earth.

Stephen says – 'my main guide is a gentleman called Archie May. Archie was a soldier, killed, I think, in the First World War. I suspect he may have been blown up or badly shot in the left arm, which is why my own arm becomes interlocked before I start my clairvoyance. As soon as the arm starts constricting, then I know that Archie is with me, and I start to relax, although it isn't always comfortable leaping across the stage like Quasimodo. The arm goes very cold, and I hate anyone touching it, but as soon as the communications are finished, everything immediately goes back to normal.

'Archie is a very serious man – he doesn't say very much – but what he does do is act a bit like a master of ceremonies. In any one evening I can be dealing with as many as fifteen different guides, all trying to link with me on behalf of their own people in spirit and on the earth plane, and Archie keeps them all in order for me. He usually makes his presence felt ten or fifteen minutes before I go out to start a demonstration, but there are times when he's a bit late and I have to walk out on to the stage all by myself. This is scary, believe me, but I go out there with blind faith in the fact that even if he is a bit late he'll get to me before I've got to start bringing the messages through, and he's never let me down yet. I'm aware of the audience, a sea of faces, all expecting me to work miracles and pull rabbits out of a hat, but there are no miracles and there are certainly no rabbits. Just me and Archie and the people from the world of spirit. I'm nervous – I mean, how could I not be? But at the same time I'm filled with these fantastic feelings of love, because if there is one thing that binds *all* the spirit people together it is the feeling of love that they have for the friends and relatives they've left behind.

'Archie isn't my only guide – just the main one. There are numerous others, all of whom work on different levels of spiritual vibration, each communicating with spirits on different levels of understanding. There's a young lad called Christopher who helps me link with children who have passed over, and there's a black guy called Warren who helps me link with suicides or people who have known great distress and trouble in their lives. I suspect this is because Warren must have had these kind of experiences himself while he was down here – I certainly think he must have spent some time in a prison cell because a lot of the people he helps me link with have either been in prison or have had a lot of problems with the law.

'There are many many others, but I can't always put a name to them. My main guide is definitely Archie, and without him I'd feel very vulnerable and lost.'

'Has he always been with you?' I asked.

'No, not at all. I first experienced his presence in the early nineties. I was demonstrating at Rotherham arts centre and it was one of the most brilliant nights I'd ever had to date. I'd been aware of this soldier energy up on the platform with me, but it wasn't until I'd come off stage at the end of the evening that someone told me my arm had gone all crooked and funny.

'There were some *great* messages that night, although, do you know, I can't recall a single one. I do know that I went home on an all time high, and slept like a baby. I woke up the following morning at the crack of dawn with Archie's voice in my ear, and it gave me the most fantastic feeling of reassurance and positive energy. I remember that I went out and did a whole day's gardening and got a tremendous amount of work done without evening breaking into a sweat.'

An interesting thought crossed my mind on the subject of Archie May. While it might be very difficult to research and prove the existence of a Red Feather or a Brown Owl, it should not be impossible to trace the existence of an English army sergeant killed in action on the Western front, circa 1917-1918. This is on hold as a possible book project for the future, so watch this space!

'Can you,' I asked 'make contact with your guides or do you have to wait for them to make contact with you?'

'Before I go out on stage I ask them for their help, and when I've finished I'll thank them for the part they've played, but basically, no, it's a one way communication.'

'What about when you're *not* on stage? Do they make contact with you in your every day life?'

'Yes they do, but only very occasionally, and not necessarily in an obvious way. I remember a few years ago I was travelling somewhere on a train and there was this lady sitting opposite me. She was in her mid-thirties, quite attractive, but she seemed to be very sad and depressed. I don't know when I first became aware of him, but there was suddenly a little coloured boy, about nine years old, sitting next to her, looking up at her with these enormous brown eyes filled with love and adoration. He kept glancing at me – he never said anything, but it was almost as though he was willing me to say something to the lady.

'I wasn't on the stage and I don't make a habit of striking up conversations with strange people, but as it happened we both got out at the same station, and as the lady was walking up the platform steps ahead of me I just felt that I had to say something. So, I caught her up and politely introduced myself, and asked her if she might know anything about a little coloured boy who wanted to tell her how much he loved her.

'I have to say that she gave me a very strange look and wanted to know why I was asking her this question, so I had to explain that I'd seen the little boy sitting with her on the train, and how unhappy he was because *she* seemed to be so unhappy. At this point the lady softened and told me that she'd lost her adopted son the year before, who indeed had been a little coloured chap, and that he had just been nine years old when he'd passed over. Because that particular week was the anniversary week of his death, she'd been sitting there with him very much on her mind. We went our separate ways and I never saw her again, but I'd like to think I might have helped a little bit.

'Then there was another time when I was still only about seventeen – still with long curly hair and my ear ring – and I'd gone across to this psychic fair in York. I'd been doing a lot of readings that year, and felt that I wanted to have a reading myself from someone – not that I needed one for any particular reason, just because I wanted to hear what someone else might have to say.

'There was this one reader, a lady called Betty Nugent, and I sat with her because all the other readers were busy. We'd barely got started when I suddenly felt very sick, and then, whoosh, I was out of myself, floating above the ground and looking down at my own body. I could see Mrs Nugent talking to me – her lips were moving but I couldn't hear anything – then I finally managed to blurt out "I'm floating! I'm floating!" and then I blanked out for a minute. When I came round I was still floating in the air, but what was worse was the fact that I couldn't move a muscle to help myself. I think I did manage to tell her that I couldn't move, and very gently she talked me down, first of all telling me to move my feet, and then my legs, and bit by bit I settled back into my own body.

'Apparently, Mrs Nugent had come to the fair hoping to have a reading herself but everyone had been too busy. She'd needed some reassurance from her late husband, and seeing the opportunity, her husband had used me to get a message across. Apparently, while I was out of the world in a trance state, Mrs Nugent's husband used my vocal chords to tell Mrs Nugent what she needed to hear and according to Mrs Nugent the information that came out of my mouth while I was blacked out was very accurate, even down to the description of a holiday cottage she'd used a few weeks before with a door that was only four feet high.

'Mrs Nugent was very pleased, but afterwards I felt awful. It had been a very frightening and unprecedented experience. I hadn't known what was happening and I'd been totally out of control. I remember I went round to Jane McDonald's home that evening – and this was long before she became famous, of course – and I made a pact with the spirit world that if they ever pulled a stunt like that again, I would quit and that would be the end of it.'

'Has anything like that ever happened again?' I wanted to know.

'No, they've kept their promise – or at least I think they have. It's hard to be objective because over the years I've learned to maintain a lot more control. If the experience with Mrs Nugent had happened yesterday, for example, I'd have known how to handle it and wouldn't have been so phased out.'

I decided at this point in the conversation to change the subject. 'Do you want to tell me a bit more about your friendship with Jane McDonald?'

Stephen laughed out loud but his eyes remained hard and cautious. 'Yes – but not without talking to her about it first...' This is typical of Stephen's unwillingness to break the slightest confidence. '...But what I *will* do is tell you about Marti Caine.'

Chapter Twelve: Miracles and Marti Caine

Marti Caine was essentially a British star, rocketing to fame in the 70's through Television's New Faces and maintaining her star status throughout the rest of her career until she died tragically of lymphoma in the mid 90's. Hers was an exceptional gift, for not only was she a very attractive lady who oozed sex appeal, she was also a highly talented singer and a comedienne who wove her way into the hearts of the British public through her numerous TV appearances and sell out shows and tours. Her raw self deprecating humour tickled the nation's funny bone, and such was her personality and the nature of her presentation that it was impossible not to like her. She battled valiantly against the cancer that killed her (just as she had battled for recognition around the Northern clubs for so many years long before she became famous) and she wrote a witty and laconic book about her fight with the insidious disease that finally claimed her life

A couple of years after she had passed over, Stephen was rattling along the M62 in his E Type Austin Maestro when – 'All of a sudden the car was filled with this fantastic spiritual presence and this woman's voice told me that she was Marti Caine and that she was going to help both me and Jane McDonald, but first I would need to read her book. Well, I knew the name Marti Caine, but I really didn't know anything too much about her, or who she was, or how she'd died, and I certainly wasn't aware that she'd written a book. I filed the incident away in my mind, but I didn't speak about it to anyone. There have been too many mediums claiming contact with the stars, including Elvis and even Princess Diana, and I didn't want people thinking I was a member of this particular club. I made a mental note that I would try to get her book, but then, probably because I was incredibly busy at that time, I promptly forgot all about it.

'Anyway, about a month later I was scheduled to do a demonstration in Blackpool, and for some silly reason I got there much too early, so to kill time I went and wandered around this charity jumble sale. I was thumbing through the old books, and lo and behold, there was Marti's book vibrating away in my hands, so I bought it there and then for the princely sum of ten pence, and it lived in the glove compartment of the car for ages before I got round to reading it. When I finally *did* get round to opening the book I was in for a shock. A piece of paper fell out from between the pages advertising a church event at which the guest speakers were advertised as J. Holbrook and S. McDonald. All right, I know the initials were the wrong way round, but something like that has got to be more than coincidence, hasn't it?

'What I couldn't figure out at the time was why Marti Caine would particularly want to help me and Jane.'

As an impartial observer I can see exactly why Marti Caine might want to help someone like Jane McDonald. Like Marti, Jane is an excellent vocalist who uses her personality with great power to communicate her talent. Like Marti Jane's roots are in the bloody cut and thrust world of the Northern club circuit, and like Marti, Jane was relatively unknown until she got one lucky TV break. The two women have a common bond of experience and heritage.

Stephen doesn't like doing personal readings any more, but when she was at a low point in her life a few years ago Jane asked him if he could pick anything up for her and immediately he tuned in to a confused vision of a TV documentary set on board some sort of ship where there'd be some kind of competition between Jane and four or five other people. At the time the vision made little sense but within a year Jane had emerged as the star of the TV programme "The Cruise". More latterly Stephen predicted she would be hosting a 'new faces kind of talent show on peak time television' – which Jane subsequently did with great aplomb and success, and, of course, it was exactly the kind of show that brought Marti Caine into the public eye back in the 70's. Link complete, game set and match.

Why Marti might want to help Stephen in particular has been a little bit more obscure until very recently.

In March of this year (2000) Stephen wife's Caroline was diagnosed as having lymphoma – the very same illness that lifted Marti across the footlights into the great eternal theatre of the afterlife.

Both Stephen and Caroline are incredibly positive people and with all the love and empathy from their many many friends and supporters, they are fighting brilliantly against this little known disease that can be so dreadful.

It also stands to reason that all of Stephen's spiritual friends and allies will be rallying round to help, no doubt led by the irrepressible and incorrigible Miss Marti Caine who promised to be of special help to Stephen all those years ago on the M62.

As with much prophesy, it made little sense then, but it makes a lot of sense now.

As a matter of course, in the process of writing this book, I pass on the rough drafts of each chapter to Stephen before correcting them, tidying them up etc., and sending them off via snailmail to the printers down in Cornwall. This next section of chapter twelve I have deliberately held back from my good buddy because if he were to read it, he would cringe with embarrassment and exercise his power of veto – and yet the next bit is important first to understand why I have committed myself to this project and secondly for you to understand something of the true measure of the man.

I was brought up in the highly disciplined and autocratic atmosphere of the *old* theatre where the motto "the show must go on" was written in blood on tablets of stone and adhered to as a fundamental principle of life. Thus, whether or not I am their greatest fan, I bow my head in homage to people like

Tommy Cooper who walked on to the stage one night, full well knowing that his chances of walking off it alive were fairly minimal.

...To master magician David Nixon who was told that his wife and children had been killed in a car crash – just five minutes before he was due to walk out and do a live broadcast of his very popular TV show back in the early 60's. He did the show and only collapsed with grief afterwards.

...To Roy Orbison whose wife and children perished in a catastrophic house fire the very day he was scheduled to perform in Nashville, Tennessee. The Big 'O' did the show first and buried his family afterwards.

You could argue that this is taking "the show must go on" philosophy to the extreme, but it is my heritage and my philosophy: I understand it, respect it, and admire it.

On the very day that Caroline's lymphoma was diagnosed Stephen demonstrated to a full house in Liverpool and delivered one of the most brilliant evenings of clairvoyance I've ever seen him deliver. I know that he was feeling incredibly low and desperately frightened, but not for one minute did he let this get in the way of what he saw as his duty to his audience. It was neither arrogance nor showmanship, but sheer professionalism and dedication.

Stephen gives little of himself away, either on stage or off it, and he has always made a point of keeping his private family life a long way distant from his professional public life. It is some indication of his emotional state that night, that at the *end* of the evening he did actually announce to his audience that his wife was very ill, and therefore, rather than hanging around to chat and answer questions, he hoped people would understand if he left straight away so that he could be back at his wife's hospital bedside for midnight.

There were 196 people in the audience at the Liverpool Moat House Hotel, and to date this office has received get well cards or telephone calls of support from more than 150 of those people. Liverpool – Stephen thanks you very much!

96

There is a vital postscript to this chapter, and it is in this postscript that we will talk about miracles.

After feeling ill for many weeks, Caroline Holbrook was hospitalised on March 18th and a growth was discovered in the lymph glands of her throat. A biopsy sample was taken on the 18th, and on the 19th the result of the biopsy clearly and unambiguously showed cancerous cells, indicating beyond all shadow of reasonable doubt that she was suffering from lymphoma.

Nineteen days later Caroline underwent surgery and the growth in the lymph gland was removed. However, when first a tissue sample and then the growth en'total was sent for biopsy, there was absolutely no trace at all whatsoever of any cancerous cells.

Caroline's medical team scurried back to the original biopsy report and double checked everything, and putting things in a nutshell, on 19th of March Caroline had lymphoma, but by April 8th she hadn't. The medical team had no cohesive explanation for this turn of events, although they were adamant that on neither occasion has there been an incorrect diagnosis. When Stephen, confused and bewildered, half daring to hope that there might be some reprieve, asked for some kind of explanation, Caroline's specialist looked him in the eye and raised her hands in supplication, saying: *"Mr Holbrook, what can I tell you? Your wife DID have lymphoma and now she doesn't! As to the cause of this, I have to cast a very wide net!"*

For many long weeks after this second diagnosis both Stephen and Caroline held their breath. During the spring and early summer Caroline had two detailed CAT scans, the first showing nothing, the second registering 'a very slight shadow adjacent to one of her ovaries' – but of the dreaded lymphoma, no signs at all.

So what happened? The logical explanation is that the medical authorities got it wrong and there was a misdiagnosis on the 19th of March. This seems far more logical than to assume that three subsequent major tests have all been flawed. However the medical authorities are insistent that no mistake was made in the March 19th biopsy, and they have their records to prove it.

Giving the medical team the benefit of the doubt, which it seems fair enough to do in the circumstances, what other explanation can there be for this sudden turn of events and dramatic change of fortune?

There is an explanation, which although it may sound incredible is not without precedent and all I can tell you is what I think has happened.

Within hours of the March 19th diagnosis a well-meaning friend circulated Caroline's photograph around just about every spiritualist church in the North of England and she was immediately put on the church's "healing list." Furthermore, as has already been said, there is a phenomenal amount of goodwill directed at Stephen through the honesty and the integrity of his work. Friends, colleagues, fellow spiritualists, all the thousands of people he has helped over the years have been praying for him and wishing him well...

From the Earthplane, then, a holistic petition will have been salvoed on the wings of a communal prayer to the world of spirit – and I am convinced that spirit heard the prayer and responded favourably.

I am equally convinced that the spiritual entity of Marti Caine was closely present throughout these proceedings shepherding all of Stephen's spiritual allies to Caroline's bedside and I further believe that during the period between March 19th and April 8th there was spiritual intervention and psychic surgery in the case of Caroline Holbrook.

As I have said, this sort of thing is *not* without precedent and there are many cases (and a number of very authoritative books available) on the subjects of absent healing, angelic intervention and psychic surgery.

Stephen is humbled by the thought that something of this magnitude might have happened in Caroline's case, but for want of any better or more logical theory, he is slowly and hopefully beginning to accept that something of this nature might have happened.

For myself, I am quietly convinced that it has.

Stephen – on Stephen and Caroline

I laugh when people ask me if I've got any hobbies because half the time I've got to check my diary to see when I've got time to wash my hair! My life is totally dedicated to my work and to my family and I'm so lucky to have the love and support of my wife Caroline... Let me tell you a bit about Caroline...

When I first met her, I have to admit I didn't go for her personality, I went for her looks. She was totally stunning, and she still is. I know this must sound a bit shallow, but I was very young! Over the years this has changed, of course, but when I was just a lad I thought that if someone looked good they were automatically a nice person. Bloodyhell, how wrong you can be sometimes – but I wasn't wrong with Caroline!

I suppose it's the Taurean in me. I like nice things, and I was so proud to be going out with this beautiful girl... She'd got this short cropped white blond hair, always had a fantastic make-up job, always wore the right gear – she was like a model who'd stepped out of the pages of a Vogue catalogue...

We met in a nightclub called The Pussy Cat. I saw her across the room and thought "oh my God she's absolutely gorgeous, but there's no way a girl like that could be interested in someone like me." I kept expecting to see her with some Chippendale type Adonis, but she kept looking over at me, and I kept looking behind me to see who she was looking at! When we did get chatting we realised that we were both hairdressers and spent the whole evening talking about each other's hair!

At first the attraction was just a physical thing, but then I began to realise it was all a big front and behind it all she wasn't at all confident... She always thought she was fat and she hid behind a mask. In a way I felt that I was there to bring her out of herself... And now, after fifteen years of ups and downs, we've found a much deeper level of mutual understanding. I love her now more than ever. We've found that rare quality of harmony, and my love for her grows with every passing day...

I remember the first house we bought. It was a one up one down box and it cost us all of fourteen grand. Our first proper holiday, just after we'd bought the house, was in Scarborough... We spent the week on the beach and in the prize bingo parlour! We saved up all our winning tickets so that we could furnish our little home and at the end of the week we went back loaded down with a duvet, an alarm clock, sheets, pillow cases, a bean bag, cutlery, crockery, even a tea pot... We actually managed to fit out our house, and all the stuff matched because it came from the same bingo palace...

Chapter Thirteen: A Haunting In Transit

Dave Munroe eyed the old white Transit van with equal degrees of love and loathing. It stood forlornly in the corner of the car park beneath a willow tree; the weeping branches of the tree leaned forwards in supplication to caress the rust streaked metal work of the battered old vehicle and in the twilight of the late afternoon it looked desolate and abandoned. The once bright red lettering advertising DT's Mobile Discos had faded to dull orange and not even the occasional ray of weak spring sunshine that strained valiantly to make its presence felt after a day of heavy April showers could do much to alleviate the atmosphere of depression, both in the pay and display car park and in Dave Munroe's troubled young heart.

Once, that old white van had represented a rare quality of fun and camaraderie – there had been many an impromptu party within the intimacy of its cargo section, many miles had been travelled with strings of risqué jokes causing gales of laughter that had drowned out the sound of empty lager cans clattering around the footwells: Dave had lost his virginity sprawled out on a blow up lilo wedged between the disco speakers and as such the old van was a vehicle that represented the rites of passage from boyhood to manhood... But all that, of course, was in the past and things were very different now.

Knowing that it was still too early to pick up his girl friend Debbie, but shivering in the cool of the evening, Dave marched over to the Transit, climbed in behind the wheel and turned on the engine. It chugged rather than roared into life, and while the engine warmed up, he sat and smoked a cigarette replaying the events of the past five weeks over and over again in his mind and wondering what he was going to do next. Tony, his partner in DT's Mobile Discos would have known, but Tony was dead – killed in a street brawl the previous month outside a back street nightclub in Leeds.

102

That was the official story anyway, but the truth of the matter was that no one really knew for sure exactly what had happened.

On the night in question Dave and Tony had finished their gig early – Dave had driven Debbie back to her home in Knaresborough while Tony, who was between girl friends, had decided to go clubbing. Apparently there had been some kind of altercation in the club bar between Tony and a couple of guys – no one knew the cause, but (and Dave squirmed uncomfortably at the thought) Tony could be a bit aggressive and a tad too cocky for his own good, especially after having had a few drinks, and it didn't stretch Dave's imagination too far to visualise any one of half a dozen circumstances in which Tony could have found himself in an argument with someone.

According to the club's manager, this particular argument had been carried out onto the street which was when somebody had shoved a knife between Tony's ribs and somebody else had bludgeoned him around the head with a *"blunt instrument, probably a crow bar or tyre lever"* and Tony was dead in the gutter even before the ambulance had been summoned.

'What a way to go!' Dave muttered bitterly out loud. He lit another cigarette, full well knowing that it was bad for this health, but enjoying it none the less. Even if he hadn't enjoyed it, he would still have smoked it as a gesture of defiance. Besides, if you could get killed by a crow bar when you were still only twenty four, what did a few cigarettes matter when you were still only twenty three?

After the funeral Dave had cancelled all the DT gigs, but most of the gear was still stashed in the back of the van, mainly because there was no where else to put it. He supposed he might as well sell it because there didn't seem to be much point carrying on the business without Tony. It had been a joint venture ever since they'd left school; they had been closer than brothers, and he had neither the heart nor the

103

enthusiasm to try going it alone. Besides which Tony had always been the driving force behind the business, booking the gigs and dazzling the audiences with his personality and his own brand of cheeky humour.

Dave blipped the throttle, threw away the cigarette, and cast a swift glance over his shoulder before ramming the gear lever into first. The back of the van was dark and cavernous and not for the first time over the past few weeks he had the impression of something watching him, lurking in the shadows. He knew it was only his imagination – *something lurking in the shadows!* It sounded like a scene from a Hammer Horror Film – but on each of the half dozen occasions when he'd felt the extra presence it had unnerved him, and now he looked even harder into the back of the van just to make sure there was nobody there. What he would have done if he *had* seen anything remained to be seen, and he bit his lip, annoyed with himself for his own temerity.

The fact that Debbie had insisted that he take her to the spook show that night didn't help much, and he became even more annoyed with himself for having capitulated to her wishes so easily. The trouble with Debbie was that she was very lovely, very sexy, very determined, and she could wind anyone, including Dave, around her little finger! All right, he was probably out of order calling a demonstration of clairvoyance a 'spook show' but that was pretty much what it was, wasn't it? Dave had no firm religious beliefs one way or the other, but one thing he was sure of was that once you were dead, you were dead, and that was it. There was no coming back – God, could you just imagine it? It would be something like that old "American Werewolf in London" movie – totally grotesque! Tony certainly wasn't coming back from the dead, and anyone who said they could talk to dead people was totally off their trolley.

That's what Dave Munroe thought then, anyway.

He could tell the moment that she got into the van that Debbie was angry with him about something, and he tentatively asked her what was wrong.

'Dave, for heaven's sake, we're going out to the theatre and you look as though you've just walked off a building site!'

He was about to say that it wasn't a proper night at the theatre, like it would be if you were going to see a play or a film – that it was only this spooky clairvoyant thing. Then, thinking better of it, he decided to keep his mouth shut, which was just as well because Debbie hadn't finished yet.

'And you're still wearing that disgusting old leather jacket – I know it was Tony's, but it was past its sell by date when he bought it second hand from Leeds market whenever it was that he bought it.' Her voice softened a little. 'Look, I know he was your friend and all that, but he's dead now and you've got to let him go.'

'If that's what you really think then why are we going to see this bloody clairvoyant thing?' he retorted angrily, not wanting to get into a fight but feeling he had to say something to defend both his appearance and his position.

To his own surprise, Debbie fell quiet for a minute, and he thought he'd scored his point. Then, in a musing tone of voice, she said: 'Umm, I suppose even you might get a message tonight, and that would change your mind about a few things, wouldn't it...?' Then, with more vehemence; 'But it still doesn't give you an excuse to look like a tramp, and after tonight, if you want me in your life, that damn jacket has got to go, and I don't care if it belonged to Tony or Uncle Tom Cobleigh an' all.'

Dave seethed in silence, but sadly resolved to consign the black leather jacket to the wardrobe next time he came to collect Debbie for a date – *if* he came again to collect Debbie for a date. And as for him getting a message from someone that was dead, that had to be the joke of the millennium!

The Fraser Theatre in Knareborough was full. This surprised Dave because he didn't think so many people would be interested in this sort of thing. He was also surprised to see that he was not the only man in the audience. Certainly, 70% of the seats were taken by women, but the rest were taken by fellers, and none of them were the old Colonel Blimp types in their dotage. Maybe, and he suppressed a secret grin, they were here for the same reasons he was – namely, just to please their womenfolk and keep them happy. At least Debbie seemed a bit more relaxed now, and with a small sigh he settled down to what he anticipated was going to be ninety minutes of acute boredom.

Dave's third surprise of the evening came when the man who did the clairvoyance thing walked out onto the stage. He'd expected to see some old duffer in an evening suit, but instead, this was quite a young guy, not much older than he was himself, with long blond hair and designer stubble, and (Oh Thank You God) dressed as casually as he was dressed himself in a pair of jeans and an open neck shirt. He hoped that Debbie might take note, and if she didn't he would make a point of mentioning it before the night was over!

He listened with half an ear while the blond guy spoke of how people didn't really die – how their bodies died, but how their spirits carried on living eternally ever afterwards – but then he lost interest when the clairvoyant started talking to a lady on the front row about someone called Harry who'd had a pet tortoise. A tortoise indeed! Maybe later on he'd wave a magic wand and the tortoise would appear on the stage reciting its two times table!

Dave Munroe had had three late nights on the trot, and he hadn't been sleeping well since Tony died anyway. The theatre was warm, and although he didn't actually doze off, he soon found himself in that half way state between sleep and wakefulness. He was brought back to full consciousness with

Debbie giving him an enormous jab in the ribs with her sharp little elbow.

'Wassup?' he hissed plaintively.

'It's Stephen!' Debbie sounded excited. 'I think he's got something for you!'

'Who's Stephen?' Dave asked blankly.

'Stephen Holbrook!' Debbie snapped irritably. 'The man on the stage, you dumbo! Will you just listen to what he's saying, for God's sake!'

Dave focused on the stage and almost, but not quite, made eye contact with the blond man who was peering into the audience as though he was looking for something he'd lost.

'I want to talk to someone,' he was saying, 'someone over this side of the theatre, who has lost either a brother or a very close friend, just in the last few weeks. This person would have died very violently, but not as the result of an accident. The link is with someone who drives a white van and I'm getting the number three very strongly. Can *anyone* take this, please? I'm also getting a letter D linking with a name like Dave or David... I *know* that someone over this side of the theatre can take this, so please talk to me, whoever you are.'

'Dave for Christ's sake, put your bloody hand up!'

Dave recoiled in shock. He'd been going out with Debbie for the better part of a year and this was the first time he'd ever heard her swear. He was also in shock from the words flowing down from the stage. *White van.* He and Tony drove a white van. *The letter D.* His name was Dave. *The number three.* Tony had been killed around three o'clock in the morning, and (Dave's stomach suddenly felt empty) the van's registration number had three three's in it. And oh hell, what was the date that Tony had died? Was it the third or had it been the second or maybe even the fourth? He couldn't think; he was floundering, but if it had been his Mum's birthday on the previous Sunday, then that meant – oh shit yes, Tony had

107

died on the third. *Brother died violently not an accident last six weeks.* Tony had been like a brother. He had died in the last six weeks. He had died violently.

Dave Munroe slowly raised his arm. 'Over here!' he called, but the call came out as a croak.

It seemed to Dave that the clairvoyant was standing directly in front of him, although in real terms, he must have been all of thirty feet away on the apron of the stage.

'Just yes or no, please sir... Can you understand the link I've got here?'

'Yes.'

'All of it or just a bit of it?'

'All of it.' There was a little more force in Dave's voice now, and the clairvoyant, who at first had seemed frustrated and impatient, began to relax.

'Right then sir, let's get this right... The person who passed over... Not your brother, but a very close friend, almost like a brother to you... Just yes or no?'

'Yes.'

'...And this person, died very violently?'

'Yes.'

The clairvoyant rubbed the back of his head. 'What I'm getting here is lots of head damage – there would have been other damage, but I'm being told that it's what happened to his head that took him over to the other side... Can you understand this?'

Dave thought of the coroner's report and answered in the affirmative.

'...And he's telling me that it wasn't an accident. He's really insistent about this. He's saying that it wasn't an accident and that he knows what you've been thinking, but it *wasn't his fault.* I know there's been a lot of speculation since he passed over and he's telling me that there's a lot yet to come out that hasn't been discovered yet. He's saying that there weren't just two of them, but four! Do you understand?'

'I... Yes... I think so...'

'And am I right in thinking in connection with whatever we're talking about here there would have been a lot of officialdom? The police? The Coroner's Office?'

'Yes.'

'It's very important that you understand what he's telling you, sir. Not two of them, but four, and that sooner or later it will come out... I'm getting the name here again that came through before... David? Dave? Who is Dave?'

'I am.'

'Right!' The clairvoyant clapped his hands and started walking up and down the stage with great energy. 'You're Dave, and your friend was killed violently about six weeks ago, and I'm getting the initial letter T... Tom, Thomas, Tommy... a name like that?'

'Tony.' There was a feeling of constriction in Dave's chest and he felt as though he couldn't breathe. Distantly he was aware of the fact that Debbie was tightly gripping his hand, and in more ways than he could imagine he found this to be incredibly encouraging.

'Tony... Right sir, just yes or no... Would you understand what he meant if he said that you haven't come to terms yet with what's happened, and that you're still all at sixes and sevens with yourself, because you're not sure what you should be doing?'

'Yes. I understand that.'

'Good, well Tony's telling me that you've got to carry on by yourself, and.... Sir, I am right in thinking that you've got a white van, aren't I? And it would be quite a big van, wouldn't it? Something like a Ford Transit?'

'Yes, it's a Ford Transit.'

'And you came in it tonight? And you came with someone – not just on your own?'

'Yes, that's right.'

The clairvoyant stopped pacing and his voice modulated onto a lower, almost teasing tone. 'Tell me this though sir – when you're in the van on your own, have you had the feeling that there's been someone there with you?'

Dave's blood ran cold. 'Yes... I have had that feeling. A couple of times...'

'Well, you've been right because your mate Tony's been there with you coming along for the ride, and he's with me now, telling me... Yes,' the clairvoyant turned and spoke over his shoulder almost as though there was someone there standing on the stage next to him, 'yes, I'll tell him that... He's telling me sir, something about a coat... Can you understand why he might be telling me something about a coat or has there been an argument, just recently, about a coat – no – not a coat, but a jacket, a black leather jacket?'

Suddenly there was a lightening in Dave's body and he felt like he wanted to laugh and cry at the same time. 'Yes, I know about the jacket,' he said to confirm the clairvoyant's link. 'As a matter of fact, I'm wearing it!'

There was some laughter from the audience which reminded Dave that he was sitting in a room full of people who were hanging on to his every word.

'But, and let me see if I've got this right, it was originally Tony's jacket?'

'Yes.'

'And would I be right in saying you've just been thinking about selling something?'

'Yes.'

'Well, Tony's telling me it's got to be your decision but he hopes that you don't. Who is Robert?'

'Uh, I don't know?

'I'm getting someone called Robert who passed over two or three years ago... It would have been in a car crash, but not in this country. Somewhere abroad. Possibly tying in with a holiday?'

'Sorry I don't know...'

'I do! I do!' a voice called out three or four rows behind.

'Right, got it... Sir I've got to leave you now and say goodnight and God bless, I hope you can use the evidence, and just remember what Tony's told you... He says he wasn't ready to go, and he never thought that he'd be talking to you in a place like this tonight, but he's very pleased that he's managed to make the link with you and whatever you decide to do, he'll be watching over you from the other side, and if you do get the feeling that there's someone riding around in that white van with you, don't worry, it's only Tony hitching a lift...'

The clairvoyant went on to talk to a lady about her husband called Robert who had died in a car crash in Tenerife three years before, leaving Dave Munroe sitting silent and stunned by the enormity of what had just happened.

As a postscript to this chapter, I introduced myself to Dave Munroe at the end of the evening, and although still in some state of shock, he did agree to talk to me a few weeks later. As a result of that meeting I have written this chapter entirely from his point of view.

He is aware of the fact that something "very mysterious and amazing" happened in The Frazer Theatre, but is still not absolutely certain that there is an afterlife or that it is possible to communicate with spirits. Equally, he is at a loss to explain how Stephen Holbrook was able to provide the messages that he received. On a practical note, he has arranged for the Transit van to be re-sprayed and he intends to start gigging with the mobile disco later in the year. He still wears Tony's leather jacket "pretty well most of the time" – but not when he's out on a date with Debbie.

Chapter Fourteen: Mental Telepathy?

I liked Dave Munroe and I take this opportunity to thank him for his candour in relating the events that have provided me with chapter thirteen of this book. At the same time I am both amazed and a little disappointed that despite the plethora of evidence he still finds it difficult to believe in the concepts of life after death and spiritual communication. When I told him as much he suggested that Stephen might have been able to do what he did through the powers of telepathy, and in an odd way this provided me with some food for thought.

I am not unfamiliar with the concept of mental telepathy – indeed I spent many years in the 1980's researching and experimenting with this phenomena with some startling but inconsistent results – but just to be sure of my own terms of reference I looked the word up in the Concise Oxford Dictionary, and I quote: *Telepathy: the supposed communication of thoughts or ideas otherwise than by the known senses.*

Therefore, by the letter of definition when Stephen is demonstrating his talents as a medium he is functioning as a telepath and when I am sitting at my own table of psychism, an element of telepathy also comes into my own work insofar as ideas and thoughtforms are being communicated without the aid of the spoken word. In my case, I am not certain where the information comes from – I speculate and I suppose, but I do not actually *know*. On the other hand there is no such ambiguity in Stephen's mind: the messages and information he receives comes from the spiritual presence of people who have passed over from this life to the next. This is his absolute conviction and belief and the evidence lends itself whole-heartedly to this conviction.

Therefore when Dave Munroe says Stephen's talents could be based on telepathy there is an element of the truth in his supposition, but if he is really suggesting that Stephen Holbrook is a mind reader who can reach out from the stage or the platform and pick up random thoughts from members of his audience and then develop them into individual psychodramas that very conveniently fit into a person's own unique experiences of bereavement and emotional loss, then this is clearly preposterous.

What might be in the minds of a two hundred strong audience and what would a so called "mind reader" pick up in such circumstances?

Logically the thoughts of an audience would revolve around business deals, relationships, new cars, new homes, money worries and aspects appertaining to health. Yes, if they had knowingly come to what had been advertised as an evening of clairvoyance there would be an undercurrent of expectation and hope – *is this man really what he says he is, and if so will I be able to get a message from my Mum?* – but the anomaly is that Stephen very seldom brings messages through that have anything to do with cash and careers or an individual's romantic or sexual agendas, and even when he does, they only connect peripherally with the recipient's own ambitions and are inevitably much more deeply concerned with the nature of the relationship between the recipient of the message and the person who has passed over who, through Stephen, is sending it   Stephen is adamant that he is not a mind reader and offers the following thoughts…

'Look, if I was just a mind reader and I was reading the minds of the audience, I'd get it right every time, and I'd pick up everything that was on that person's mind. Now they might be thinking of their Mum or their Dad, but they'd be thinking other things too – only I never get those other things, which surely I would if I was just reading minds or doing tricks with mental telepathy.

'And there's something else you've got to think about here. Sometimes I'll be talking to someone in the audience and they won't have a clue about what I'm going on about. I had a link with this lady a few weeks ago, and I was being told that she should be wearing her Grandmother's locket.

The lady said that to the best of her knowledge her Grandma, who'd only passed over to the other side a few weeks previously, had never had a locket, or if she did, she had no knowledge of it, and it certainly had never been given to her.

'But I had the Grandmother on stage with me and she was going on and on about this locket, and that it had to be given to the lady in the audience who was her Granddaughter, and that it was so important that the locket should be found and worn because there was a vitally important message connected with it. All I could do was impress these thoughts on the lady in the audience and ask her to go home and have a search through Granny's things, and at least remember what she'd been told.

'Anyway, about a week later I had a phone call from this lady to say that she had been going through her Grandmother's sewing box, which wasn't the normal place you'd expect to find a piece of jewellery, and there on the bottom of the box was the locket with a broken clasp. Inside the locket was a small photograph of the Grandmother holding a tiny baby which subsequently turned out to be my lady in the audience only a few days after she'd been born, and on the back of the locket, inscribed in the silver, were the words "with love"

'The lady is now wearing the locket which has made her Grandma very happy, and in her own way, she has got her message through. Saying to someone 'I've got a message here from your Grandmother who says she loves you very much' is one thing, but to be able to prove it in a hard tangible way is another thing entirely, and it seemed to me that Granny's spirit wanted to give her Granddaughter that degree of proof.

'There was another occasion when I was talking to this chap about a link with a brother in Canada. He really took me to task and gave me a hard time, declaring that first of all he had no links with Canada, and certainly he didn't have a brother. I remember it was extremely embarrassing because the link was so strong and I just couldn't let it go, but this guy was adamant that I was wrong and it was clear from his attitude that he thought I was conning him.

'The better part of a year went by, when out of the blue this chap phoned me up to apologise. He said he'd just received a letter from a law firm in Vancouver informing him that his brother, a brother he'd never known he had, had died the previous year and it had taken the law firm the better part of fourteen months to trace the next of kin. This had opened a whole can of worms, because when he'd started digging around in the family history books he learned to his shock that not only did he have a brother but there was a sister somewhere too, and all three children had been separated and adopted as babies.

'These are just a couple of incidents, but there have been scores of occasions when something like this has happened. They haven't had a clue what I've been trying to tell them, but then a few days or a few weeks later there's been a phone call or a letter to tell me that this or that has been found or something or another has happened and the message now makes perfect sense.

'So basically, if there are times when I know things about the person who is getting the message that they don't know about themselves, how can I be reading their minds?'

If we take the case of Dave Munroe and sift through the evidence of the link, one clear fact does emerge.

Immediately prior to the evening of clairvoyance at the Fraser Theatre in Knaresborough Dave had been thinking about his dead friend and the tragic circumstances in which he had died. He had been feeling lost and at a loss about what to do with his life. He had been nervous about an unknown 'presence' in the back of the white Transit van. He had been thinking about selling the mobile disco equipment. He had been wearing his dead friend's leather jacket and there had indeed been something of an argument with Debbie appertaining to this fact.

115

These were all things, which to his credit, Stephen accurately picked up on, and which, if he was just a mind reader, he might readily have plucked from Dave Munroe's head for these had been Dave's conscious thoughts.

But he hadn't been sitting there thinking 'Hey I'm Dave and my dead best friend's name was Tony, a name that sounds a bit like Tommy, which begins with the letter T.' He was not consciously thinking about the number three, and he was not consciously thinking about the coroner's report or the actual number of assailants that had laid his friend low... Which, of course, were all things Stephen also picked up on.

When I telephoned Dave Munroe yesterday to ask him if there was anything else on his mind that night, something which perhaps Stephen had made no mention of, there was a pause on the 'phone and then a chuckle – 'Yeah, I was thinking very strongly about getting laid – and thinking that things were pretty great between me and Debbie, despite the silly row about the jacket, and I was thinking about buying an engagement ring and wondering if I should ask her first or whether I should just go out and get it and give it to her as a surprise... '

So these things were also in Dave's mind, but Stephen made no mention of them at all, indicating to my way of thinking that Stephen's link was selective and unique to the spiritual vibration of Tony's presence in the theatre.

It's a sorry admission but I think that many men, by their very nature and their upbringing – not to mention macho peer group pressure – tend to resist the world of the supernatural and by definition the concept of spiritualism. Part of this is fear, part of it is arrogance, and part of it is downright ignorance and stupidity. Women, on the other hand, are far more intuitive and sensitive and thus are more able to accept abstract concepts.

Millions of words have been written in thousands of books about the difference between the sexes so I'm not going

116

to add to this great body of work by voicing my own opinions and theories – suffice to say that had Stephen's message been for a *woman* I don't think she would have had as much difficulty in accepting it at its face value as seems to have been the case with Dave Munroe. This is not to say that all men are insensitive bricks, for indeed many of the world's greatest psychics and seers and spiritual pioneers *have* been men, but sadly chaps, we are seriously outnumbered and for every man with an open heart and an open mind there are hundreds of dodos and dinosaurs.

But it isn't just men who are sceptical. Women *do* fall into this category as well, and an incident which occurred at Doncaster Civic Theatre a few years ago is a case in point. Stephen was in fine fettle, rattling his messages through with machine gun accuracy, and sitting in the audience was fellow medium Sue Cunningham and her partner. Directly in front of Sue was a woman in a red dress who kept muttering, not only to herself but to anyone within earshot "It's a plant – it's a plant!" every time Stephen brought a message through. In the end the woman in the red dress got up to leave the theatre, but no sooner had she reached the aisle when Stephen broke the link he had with someone else, and zoomed directly in on her...

'Hang on, my love, don't leave just yet because I've got a message coming through for *you!* I've got a gentleman here with only one leg, who says he is your brother.'

This stopped the lady in the red dress in her tracks and to all intents and purposes all the colour drained from her face – for indeed she did have a brother in the spirit world who had lost a leg as part of the injuries which had killed him. Stephen fired a barrage of information at her, all of which was accurate, but his coup d'etat was to mention that she had been visiting someone in prison that very same afternoon, that she had gone with her daughter, and the person being visited was her son-in-law. Stephen was quite adamant that the son-in-

117

law should not be in the prison and that he was not guilty of the crime of which he had been convicted – which had been his family's contention all along.

At the end of the evening, the woman in the red dress (who had retaken her seat and had sat riveted through the rest of the performance) approached Stephen in private and confirmed all the evidence she had been given, and more importantly told him just how much his message had hardened her and her daughter's resolve to carry on fighting for her son-in-law's early release.

This is not a unique scenario. Many people have entered a Stephen Holbrook demonstration filled with scepticism but have exited with enough hard evidence to change their minds once and for all. This is why Stephen (and I) welcome sceptics to the demonstrations. All we ask is that you consider the evidence with objectivity and an open mind and come to your own conclusions on the strength of what you see and hear.

Chapter Fifteen: The Christian Predicament

Part of promoting any show, especially when you are working on a very limited budget, is the distribution of posters and flyers. "Flyposting" – the act of sticking a poster to a wall or hoarding – is highly illegal, although once the poster is up on the said wall or billboard, by the letter of the law, you're in the clear. It's the actual *act* of putting it up which is illegal, and if you get caught in the act, the fine can be as much as £1000. Such is the stupidity and absolute silliness of this particular bit of British legal rubbish.

Having been once caught in this way (promoting a charity event for The Princess Diana Memorial Fund) I have become very circumspect, and when promoting Stephen have evolved a system whereby I walk into a shop or business premises and say something along the lines of... "Hi, I wonder if I could give you this small poster. If you can display it, that would be great, but even if you can't at least I'll know that *you* know about the event, and perhaps you'll help us spread the word." This is usually effective and frequently leads to an interesting chat with the shop assistant or the proprietor. Sometimes, however, things can go horribly wrong, such as they did in Newark a few weeks ago.

I walked into this small haberdashery with my bundle of bright yellow leaflets and approached the late middle aged lady behind the counter in my usual non-threatening way. She seemed very amiable and friendly – until she saw the poster and what it was advertising – at which point her demeanour changed instantly from one of polite interest to one of vitriolic loathing and contempt.

'We do NOT advertise clairvoyants in this shop,' she snarled. 'We're Christians!'

The expression on her face indicated quite clearly that she thought I was spawn of The Devil, and sadly I shoved the posters back into my briefcase and made my exit from the shop. Part of me wanted to stay and talk to her – to explain who Stephen was and what we were doing, and to reassure her that we were absolutely no threat to her convictions and beliefs, but another part reminded me that I had met this kind of person many many times before and there would be nothing I might say that could shift her from her position of bigotry and ignorance.

The haberdasher is not alone in taking this stance, and far too frequently over the years I have argued with members of the Christian faith, sometimes in private debate and frequently in public debate as well, but never once have I persuaded a Christian of this evangelical persuasion that there might be other routes to the Throne Room of God other than by the pathway dictated by Jesus of Nazareth.

Like many children of my age, I went to church and Sunday school, was baptised (don't remember it) and at fourteen confirmed (remember it, but didn't understand either the symbolism or the significance). As a young man I thrived on novels with a religious theme such as Lloyd C. Douglas's "The Robe" and "The Big Fisherman" and I loved those big epic movies like "Ben Hur" and "Quo Vadis" and "The Greatest Story Ever Told". My Jesus of Nazareth was a wonderfully romantic figure from the world of film and literature and His persona was strong enough in both my conscious and subconscious to push me into really reading and studying the new testament of The Bible, and in all truth there was little there to compromise my image of The Son Of God.

It was this interest that pushed me into reading *everything* of a theological nature, and this later reading made me question some of the basic tenets of the Bible's version of Jesus. Some things did not add up. There were contradictions and glaring anomalies between theology and history, all of which pushed me back into The Bible again, reading this time with less childish enthusiasm and more adult objectivity. My local vicar suggested that I didn't question things too deeply, just take The Bible quite literally for gospel, and ignore anything that anyone or anything else said – and I would be all right!

Now the enthusiastic sixteen year old might have swallowed this advice, but the objective and questioning twenty year old certainly could not.

It must also be remembered that concomitant with the above, I was also deeply interested in spiritualism and anything of a psychic nature, and it was undoubtedly the psychic and mystical side of Jesus of Nazareth that made him so interesting and appealing to me. Thus came conflict. The Church insisted that I see Jesus as God whereas I could only see Jesus as a man. The Church insisted that the only way to God was through the Godhead of Christ, whereas it was obvious to me that there were many other routes available. I became angry with The Church for its blind arrogance, and began to understand why both Islam and Judaism (not to mention anyone else who voiced an opinion that went against the Christian Church's views) have had such a problem with The Christian Church over the last two thousand years.

My Mother did her best to bring me up as a Christian but my Father was a Jew and my maternal Grandmother was a Romany gypsy born beneath the wheels of a caravan on the North Yorkshire Moors towards the end of the 19th Century. Inevitably The Church's intransigence and hypocrisy pushed me increasingly towards a resonance with my older bloodlines.

I use the word "hypocrisy" for many reasons, not least being one particular incident that occurred many years ago when I was starting out on my own pathway of psychic exploration. I was given a very hard time by one particular clergyman who upon hearing that I was "dabbling" with Tarot cards and palmistry took it upon himself to write me a five page letter of condemnation – more than a thousand words of diatribe telling me that what I was doing was an affront to God, that it was evil, that *I* was evil, and that if I didn't stop what I was doing immediately, my soul would be eternally damned. He further accused me of leading poor innocent people astray, of being at best a conman, and at worst an emissary of the Devil.

Two years later, after having gained some passing state of celebrity as a radio broadcaster and journalist, and having been high profile in the local press for raising some substantial amounts of money for a local charity, this same clergyman had the gall to phone me up and ask me if I'd do a free stint at his garden party to raise funds for his new church spire! Maybe he'd forgotten that very hateful and hurtful letter, but I had not, and I declined his kind invitation to participate.

Okay, I know I may be accused of being petty, but it was the last little straw that broke the camel's back, and since that day, I've gone my own way and have allowed the Church to do the same.

Things do change, and in the writing of this book, I wanted to know if The Church had altered its views at all. Thus, I took it upon myself to telephone my current local vicar to get some feedback. I have to say he wasn't very forthcoming – muttering about how he thought that anything of an occult nature should be left well alone. When I gently suggested that spiritualism and the occult were hardly the same thing, he said that as far as *he* was concerned they were *exactly* the same thing, but if I wanted a more eclectic answer I should contact The Diocese of York.

I duly did this and talked to a number of people before I was finally referred to Rev. Stanley Baxter who runs a Christian Healing Centre in the delightful old market town of Thirsk.

I have to say that Rev. Baxter was a welcome breath of fresh air. He told me that The Church was, in his opinion, becoming rather more tolerant in many of its views, perhaps more by force of political correctness than by any great theological conviction, but that unfortunately many members of the church at a grass roots level still found it very difficult to cast off their old prejudices. None-the-less Rev. Baxter practices aromatherapy and reflexology at his healing centre, which would have been unheard of only a few short years ago. When pressed on the specific subjects of mediumship and spiritualism, Rev. Baxter acknowledged that these subjects were a long way removed from Tarot cards etc., but still recognised that The Church tended to be very cautious and conservative in its views, and suggested that they should be left well alone or given a very wide berth. He did very kindly offer to send me a book which outlined The Church's official policy, and the book duly arrived on my mat a few days later.

The book, euphemistically titled "Deliverance" (SPCK edited by Michael Perry, ISBN0-281-04941-6) is something akin to a Christian work-book on exorcism and deals in some depth with the subjects of possession and Satanism. Given its origins and obvious allegiances, it is fairly (although not entirely) accurate in many of its assessments, and is reasonably objective in most (although again not all) of its summations and conclusions. It has to be said that if you *were* a Satanist, it would make invaluable reading if you wanted to know your enemy, and in essence, it comes over as a very honest and sincere attempt at (a) putting forward The Church's view and (b) in guiding the clergy towards a degree of knowledge and objectivity when counselling those who have had negative experiences of the paranormal and the occult.

But "Deliverance" also makes it very clear that it does not lump Spiritualism in this broad category and it acknowledges some similarity between modern day mediums and the prophets of old. Had Stephen lived in Old Testament times he might, just might, have been regarded as a prophet, unlike my poor old Grandmother, who had she lived four hundred years ago, would have been burned at the stake as a witch.

123

There is one specific section of "Deliverance" that I do take strong issue with. In the chapter on spiritualism it questions the worth and validity of messages brought through the veil by people such as Stephen Holbrook, and suggests that this is detrimental to the natural grieving process of "letting go" of a loved one.

Not only in my own experience, but also in the experience of Stephen and every other medium I've ever talked to, it is the contact between the worlds that enables and empowers the grieving party to let go, knowing that their loved ones are safe and well on the other side of the veil.

"Deliverance" also attacks the late Doris Stokes for saying "You cannot die – there is no death" and does so with a degree of cynical mischief. Of course there is *physical* death, and as anyone who has seen it "up close and personal" will acknowledge, it is seldom a pretty sight and it does always leave a scar. It's one thing to see it on a sanitised TV screen, but when it's in your face stripped of the literary dignity so frequently draped upon it, it is *not* something to be dealt with lightly.

Doris Stokes, just like Stephen and other highly tuned mediums, was highly aware of the reality of corporeal death and was making reference to the *spirit* of Man, echoing The Church's own philosophy of an afterlife to which the soul transcends after its physical demise in the human body shell. Perhaps because The Church would have us leave it there while Spiritualists take it one degree further by bringing forth *proof* of spiritual survival is the one factor which frightens The Church so much, but which also has begun to make The Christian Church sit up and take notice of what The Spiritualist Church is doing.

Sooner or later there has to be some symbiosis, some union or partnership, and it is my guess that over the next few years (all right, maybe the next few decades) The Christian Church will quietly begin to court the spiritualist movement in an attempt to find an increasing degree of common ground.

I believe that it must, because given the constant increase in the development of spiritual evolution, it is only a matter of time before there are messages filtering through from a much higher spiritual plane – this saint or that saint, possibly something of a purely angelic nature and ultimately there is no reason why there should not be a direct link with Jesus of Nazareth himself – and when those links or "that" link comes through, it will come through a clairvoyant medium and not a clergyman in his pulpit...

Unless, of course, they are one and the same.

Thus, the Christian Church finds itself in an odd predicament. On the one hand it preaches that belief in God through Jesus Christ brings us everlasting spiritual life after death, and yet at the same time it is consistently critical and fearful of the very people who can provide independent proof of this belief.

The Spiritualists are and always have been open to new ideas; their movement has constantly evolved and has never stood still. More so than most, they work very hard to disassociate themselves from the occasional rotten apple that crops up in any barrel, and in search of hard evidence for post mortem survival, they are their own most ardent critics. As I have said before, they are non-evangelical and gently embrace the concept of God's House having many mansions. They are certainly *not* critical or dismissive of other peoples' faiths, and in my own opinion, before The Christian Church draws breath to criticise spiritualism or any other alternative spiritual pathworking, it should consider long and hard on what it must do to put its own house in order.

When I talked to Stephen about Angels, he reserved judgement and when I spoke to him about reincarnation, he was rather doubtful. Now it was time to talk to him about something significantly more fundamental.

'Do you believe in God?' I asked him.

'Yes, of course I believe in God,' he answered, 'although I have no clear vision of who or what God is. I certainly don't think he's a white bearded old gentleman sitting on a throne surrounded by chubby little angels floating on fluffy white clouds!'

God, for Stephen, is a Higher Spiritual Authority, who does exert some influence over all of our lives, and because of this, God is obviously a very sentient entity and not just an amorphorous collection of energies coalescing into some indescribable jumble. Whether God loves us, or cares about us, whether he 'created' us, whether or not he, she or it is a fair God with a sense of justice, he doesn't know...

'...No, I truly don't *know* the answers to these questions, and maybe nobody can ever *know* these answers for sure, although I've met a lot of people who are pretty confident that they do have all the right answers...

'But if you're the kind of person who can believe or because you're trained to believe, or even if you have the blind faith to believe, then maybe you're lucky because you're able to build a personal relationship with God that other people can't. They say that God made Man in his own image but I've got a sneaky feeling it might be the other way round – you know, Man creating God in *his* own image.

' – Look James, I'm not a theologian, and I don't have the knowledge to give you a treatise on God. But I'd like to think I'm honest enough to appreciate what some people might call God's work – a gorgeous sunset, a beautiful dawn, a small act of kindness, you know, a neighbour helping a neighbour in a time of trouble, and things like the miracle of new babies... Then there are the big things like food getting to starving people in India or Africa, rains coming at the very last minute to put an end to long months of drought...

'Of course, the trouble is, that for every positive bright and beautiful thing, there are usually half a dozen negative things on a rising scale from a neighbour's meanness to genocide, famine, disease and war...

'This does not show God up in too kind a light, does it? So maybe God is very fair, maybe he acts as some kind of balance, but he certainly doesn't always come over as caring or loving. I suppose, to me, God is everything in nature, and maybe my vision of him is something akin to the North American Indian belief of the One Great Spirit, and when things go wrong with our world, maybe we should blame it on Man and not God, but if there *is* any truth in the concept of God making Man in his own image, then I think we might be in a spot of trouble, don't you?'

'What about Jesus?' I asked him, particularly curious to know whether his feelings on this subject came anywhere close to my own.

'Jesus obviously existed. I mean there's enough documented evidence to prove it, isn't there? Certainly as much as there is to prove the existence people like Alexander The Great, Ptolomy, Ghengis Khan, Julius Ceasar, and a whole host of other characters I could mention. So, if you can believe in *their* existence, you've got to believe in the existence of Jesus, haven't you?

'I don't have a problem in believing that this guy walked around the shores of Galilee a couple of thousand years ago, and I don't have a problem in accepting the miracles and the healings at their face value, and I don't even have a problem in accepting Jesus as *a* son of God, but I do have a problem with the immaculate conception and I do therefore have a problem seeing Jesus as the literal Son of God.

'Giving credit where credit is due, Jesus would have been a great healer, a great teacher, a great philosopher and a great hope to his followers. He would also have been a very spiritual person – a spiritualist in the truest sense of the word. Whatever else he did, he founded a world religion and if you were looking for a code of ethics by which to live your life then the Christian code is as good as any and better than most, although in all fairness, it is a difficult code and there are

127

alternatives, more suited to different people with different backgrounds and belief structures.

'I think Jesus would have been a quite remarkable person, no matter when or where he walked on this planet, but, and I've got to say this, I reckon he must have rolled over in his grave thousands and thousands of times at some of the things that have been said and done in his name!'

'Have you ever had any problems with Christians at your demonstrations?' I wanted to know, very mindful of my own experiences. 'In particular the New Age Born Again variety?'

'Oh yes, but only once or twice, and they didn't worry me too much. I believe in free speech and I've got a live and let live attitude, so if a handful of people want to come and wave banners at me, then that's their right, and I haven't got a problem with it. I might not agree with what they're saying but I'll defend to my death their right to say it. I just wish they'd show me the same courtesy and I do worry sometimes when they bully the people who are coming in to see me. I find myself wondering how *they* might feel if I came along with a load of friends to where they were trying to hold their meetings and tried to disrupt their goings on. Somehow I don't think they'd like it very much.'

Stephen suddenly guffaws with laughter and I ask him if he'll share the joke?

'I was just remembering the day we had my son Bradley baptised... Normally, I wouldn't have bothered with such a ritual, but considering that my wife's side of the family is fairly orthodox in its views, and wanting to keep everyone happy, I arranged for the local vicar to conduct the baptism. It took quite a few phone calls to get this arranged, and every time I tried to pin the vicar down to a date he seemed evasive and non-committal. After a while I twigged that he probably wasn't too keen to do this particular job bearing in mind that my posters were all over town advertising a forthcoming demonstration, and he must have thought to himself "I really don't want this kind of person coming into *my* church!"

'Anyway, the day of the Christening finally came round and we all filed into the church, and even as we were walking up the aisle towards the font the vicar was giving me these really filthy looks, and I could see he was really nervous about me being there. If he hadn't had his hands full, I dare say he might have picked up the nearest crucifix and waved it under my nose just like Peter Cushing used to do with Christopher Lee in those old Hammer horror movies.

'So, it comes to Bradley's turn to be baptised and the vicar takes him in his arms and goes through the motions, and he's just got to the bit where he says "In the name of The Father, Son and Holy Ghost I name thee Bradley Holbrook" and all the church lights started to go out, one by one, all around the building, and almost as though on cue. The vicar looks absolutely petrified, stares balefully at me, dumps Bradley back into Caroline's arms, and then does a wonderful job of fainting on the spot.

'If it hadn't been so sad, it would have been really very funny... All that had happened was that a fuse had blown and the circuit breakers had cut out one at a time just as they're designed to do, but obviously the vicar thought he should have been Christening my son Damien Omen or something.'

Stephen looks at me candidly. 'Do I really look like I'm the kind of bloke who could scare people like that?'

I have to tell him no, he doesn't – but at the back of my mind I am aware of the fact that people are always scared of the unknown or anything – or *anyone* – that is different.

I pick up on something that he said earlier and ask: 'Do you believe in miracles?'

He rubs his designer stubble chin and his eyes narrow into what, over the months of our collaboration, have become a very familiar hawk like expression. He's on his guard. Is this a trick question? Am I trying to trap him into giving something away of himself that he is not yet ready to give?

'It would depend,' he says cautiously 'on what *you* mean by the word miracle.'

I tell him, and he smiles that Holbrook half smile which always comes when he is about to share something of importance with me.

'Yes,' he says quietly and enigmatically. 'I do believe in miracles – but we won't talk about that now. Have I told you about Eric Hatton?'

Chapter Sixteen: Eric Hatton's Evidence

Eric Hatton is not only a past president of The National Spiritualist Union, he is also the Union's Honorary President and presiding president and minister of The Stourbridge Spiritualist Church. His wife is a full time medium and he has enjoyed over fifty-five years experience in the world of spiritualism. No one more than he has been responsible for guiding The Church through the latter part of the twentieth century and into the twenty first century and he is revered (and sometimes feared) throughout the movement.

He has a habit of turning up unannounced at various church meetings up and down the country and sitting quietly at the back of the hall to observe the proceedings: he will quietly make note of up and coming mediums and will bestow praise generously where it is due. On the other hand, he doesn't suffer fools gladly, and when something is wrong or is not measuring up to the Spiritualist Union's very high standards, he will come down like the proverbial ton of bricks.

This slight dapper man carries with him an air of authority that is most definitely not to be trifled with and when he turned up unexpectedly at a meeting of the York spiritualists a couple of years ago he almost, but not quite, caused havoc amongst the members. I say 'not quite' for he was recognised by one of York's leading spiritualist lights, a remarkable lady called Rose Bielby, who bade him welcome to the congregation and a little later in the evening even brought a message through for him.

Eric Hatton has seen and tested literally thousands of mediums over the years, some of whom have been good, others who have been bad, and others yet who have been very *very* good indeed.

Stephen's first meeting with Eric was slightly less than auspicious…'Back in 1997 I was invited to demonstrate at Stourbridge which was a bit of an honour because it's a very important church, and of course, I knew I'd be meeting Eric for the first time. I arrived early, trying to look my best, but my best is a very casual best. I was wearing some nice new trousers and a crisp white shirt – no, I wasn't wearing a tie, and no, I hadn't brought a jacket, because quite frankly I seldom bother with those things anyway. I deliberately got there early because I'd rather be somewhere half an hour early than five minutes late, and I was sat in one of the arm chairs in the lobby watching the congregation arrive. I won't say they looked posh, but they were all dressed a lot more formally than I was, and I began to feel a bit uneasy – you know, just a little bit *under* dressed.

'Anyway, this very smart gentleman approached me and he wasn't smiling. He looked me up and down, obviously not approving of the casual gear or the long hair, never mind the ear-ring. He said: "Do you mind if I ask who you are and what you're doing here?" There wasn't much humour in his voice, and because we'd never met, he couldn't have known who I was. Come to that, I didn't have a clue who he was either.

'I told him that I was Stephen Holbrook and that I'd come down from Yorkshire to do a demonstration for The Stourbridge Church and that I was waiting to meet Mr. Hatton.

'Then he said: "Well *I'm* Eric Hatton," and then, "Oh dear!". Nothing else, just "Oh dear!" I suppose it must have been a bit worrying for him, because let's face it, I know I don't look much like your usual medium, do I? ... And even if he'd had some good reports of the work I'd been doing in the North, I must have given him a bit of a jolt. I have to say he didn't instil me with much confidence and I remember being particularly nervous when the time came to go up on the stage. I suppose I might have stammered and stuttered a bit at first but Archie May soon took over (he was particularly strong with me that night) and I soon got into my stride.

132

'As I remember it there were some really strong links and the time just seemed to fly by. There was a great response from the audience and at the end of the demonstration Eric Hatton thanked me in public, and then he went to the trouble of thanking me again a bit later on in private. I think he was fairly impressed with me because he asked me where I'd been hiding all these years – so I told him the truth and said "Wakefield".'

They say that you can't choose your family but that you can always choose your friends. Friendship, in the purest and truest sense of the word, is a remarkable emotional bond frequently elevated and enhanced above and beyond the bounds of blood ties and family loyalties.

Sure, we all have "friends" but come on, be honest about this, how many friends do *you* have whose welfare you would put beyond that of yourself and your bloodkin? How many friends do you have that you trust implicitly? How many friends do you have who could phone you from the other side of the world and tell you that they need you there NOW because there's an emergency that only you can help them resolve – that you'd drop everything for and get on the first plane for Australia or Timbuktu? How many friends do you have who, given Sophie's Choice, would give their lives for you, and you for them? True friendship on this level is rare but it does exist, and in my own opinion and limited experience, it transcends life and time as we know it.

Mr & Mrs Eric Hatton had such a friend in Robert Hartrick. Robert, who was chairman of The Arthur Findley College in Stanstead (the HQ of The NSU) was a cheerful and flamboyant man with a tremendous sense of fun and an incredible zest for life. Eric and Robert had worked in close association for many years, bonded in the unison of their common cause. Therefore when Robert Hartrick was killed in a car accident it was not only a dreadful loss to spiritualism in general but to the Hattons in particular.

February 1994. Robert Hartrick was driving back to Stanstead Hall from Worcestershire. Three quarters of a mile from home on the ring road which circumnavigates Stanstead airport, his Jaguar hit the back of an airport coach, and Robert was killed when the car exploded in a ball of flames.

Eric Hatton was particularly distressed by his friend's untimely death, and he was also extremely curious as to the cause. The modern Jaguar is an extremely well built motor car not prone to exploding into flames no matter how hard the shunt and furthermore Robert was a highly competent and experienced driver who never drank and drove.

This element of mystery plagued Eric's mind, and as first the months and then the years passed, no light was shed upon it from either side of the grave: both Eric and Robert were committed spiritualists, and Eric found it most odd that Robert never once communicated with him.

Cut to Stourbridge Spiritualist Church some five years later when Stephen Holbrook was enjoying a return visit in the autumn of 1999. Eric introduced Stephen and then took his place on the stage. Eric's wife was sat at the very back of the packed hall, and from their different positions, they settled down to enjoy another evening of Stephen's clairvoyance.

It has to be said that neither of them was particularly thinking about Robert Hartrick; although still sorely missed with the mystery unresolved, five years had elapsed since he had passed over, and time heals most wounds eventually.

Therefore, when Stephen focused towards the back of the room and said he had something coming through from someone who had died in a fire, Mrs Hatton did not immediately make the connection. Neither, for that matter, did anyone else, but Stephen would not let it go. He paced up and down the stage in his customary caged lion mode, and then suddenly stopped, the most beatific smile crossing his face.

'Got it!' he exclaimed as though he'd just won the national lottery. 'The person who died in the fire is called

134

Robert, and it wasn't a house fire, but a fire involving a car – either a Daimler or Jaguar saloon! Now can anyone take *this* information please?'

Immediately and simultaneously both Eric and Mrs Hatton realised that this was a link for them, and once the link was forged, the amount of evidence that came through was staggering in both its depth and detail. Reference was made to dates, times, places, the subjects of private conversations between Eric and Robert, and Eric remembers feeling "absolutely amazed and totally elated."

Perhaps more importantly was Stephen's impression of what caused that dreadful car accident back in 1994... 'All of a sudden the car filled with mist and steam, completely blinding the driver. He'd braked for an emergency stop, but by then it was too late...'

Eric was deeply moved by the evidence Stephen had provided, but there was still a mystery to be solved. What would cause a car to suddenly fill up with mist to the extent that the driver could no longer see where he was going? And what about the crash itself? How was the "sudden mist" tied in with the fact that the car went up in flames upon impact, if indeed there was any such link at all between the two factors.

Some short while later Eric voiced these thoughts and questions to a friend and colleague who is an expert on fire and fire exchange systems. Eric's friend was deeply interested, and explained that he was not unfamiliar with this phenomenon. Indeed, he had recently investigated something of a remarkably similar nature.

After looking through all of the evidence, he came up with what is more than just a plausible answer.

If the car's under bonnet drain holes had become blocked with leaves and detritus, then rainwater would not be able to drain. The water levels would mount, until on cornering, the water would then cascade over the heat exchanger, and this could certainly be the cause of a sudden blast of mist being forced through the vehicles ventilation systems. In an attempt to help Eric understand what he was talking about, he conducted a simple demonstration by placing a meat tray on a stove and mixing very small amounts of water and anti-freeze. After only a few seconds there was a tremendous flash of combustion with clouds of nasty smelling steam filling the kitchen.

This story made the front page of Psychic News, but the thing that made it so important for Eric was the plethora of small personal details that came through. "There is absolutely no doubt in my mind," he told me over the telephone last week "that Stephen Holbrook had a firm and genuine link with Robert. There were things that he mentioned which made perfect sense to me, but made no sense to my wife – but then, why should they if she had not been privy to a particular conversation? And, of course, this worked the other way round as well. As I told you, I've been active in the world of spiritualism for more than fifty-five years, and I have never heard evidence so thoroughly convincing... And believe me, Mr Christie, I am not a man who can be fooled, and nor am I easily impressed."

I asked the obvious question.

"Am I impressed with Stephen Holbrook? Yes of course I am. I am both elated and flabbergasted by the strength of the messages he brought through for myself and my wife! He has a rare and wondrous gift, and, of course, at this point in time he is still so young, isn't he? If he nurtures and treasures his gifts and talents, the Good Lord alone knows what he will be capable of a few years from now."

These are Eric Hatton's words, and I have to say that they coincide totally with my own objective opinion of Stephen Holbrook's ability to communicate between two worlds.

Eric Hatton provided me with another interesting example of Stephen's ability. In Eric's own words: "That same night

Stephen brought through another message that I was personally able to corroborate. There were three young people in the audience, three cousins, who were related to me. Two members of this party had lost their Mother earlier in the year, and two years previously, they had also lost their father. In an attempt to come to terms with the loss of a father and a husband, the Mother and daughter booked a couple of weeks holiday in Tenerife.

"The two ladies enjoyed a pleasant, if slightly muted vacation, and on the day they were scheduled to return to the UK they spent the morning doing some last minute shopping, especially in the duty free shops which abound on that island. There had been some discussion as to which perfumes they should buy, and as a result, they probably bought more than they needed.

"There was still some time to kill before the coach arrived to take them to the airport, so they took two chairs by the poolside, to soak up the last of the sunshine. Only twenty minutes elapsed before the daughter realised that there was something wrong with her Mother – she was too still, and her face had gone a shade too pale beneath the recently acquired sun tan. Upon investigation the daughter was horrified to discover that her Mother was not in fact sleeping, but dead. She must have passed away in her doze with a heart attack.

"As you can imagine this was not only a double blow but also a great shock to the daughter, and having only recently buried one parent, she now had to bury another.

"I'd suggested that she might come to our church to find some solace and relaxation, and she duly arrived, but was not by any means expecting to receive a message from her Mother.

"None-the-less Stephen Holbrook did connect with her Mother, correctly identified the name of Carol and correctly diagnosed the cause of death as a heart attack whilst asleep. Initially the messages were for the third cousin, which Carol thanked profusely for being such a help in the funereal

arrangements and for being supportive towards the family –
then she turned her focus specifically onto her daughter,
commenting that at last the daughter had started using the
duty free perfume that they had bought on their last shopping
expedition together, and correctly identifying the brand name.
She also asked (through Stephen) if she remembered them
walking along the sea front on the last full day of their holiday
– the day before she died – when Carol had drawn her
daughter's attention to a man who had caught her eye in the
near distance, commenting that this gentleman looked a lot
like her late father.

"The daughter had said "No Mum, not really" but Carol
had been convinced of the resemblance. These were things
that absolutely no one other than Mother and Daughter, had
any knowledge of, and yet Stephen was providing this
information from somewhere.

"When I questioned the young lady, and believe me, I did
question her, I was able to confirm the incident on the sea
front with the man who looked like Carol's late husband, I
was also able to confirm the shopping spree for perfume and
the fact that the Daughter had indeed broken into the first
bottle that very evening prior to leaving home for the church."

I should like to take this opportunity to thank Eric Hatton for
taking so much time out to help me with this chapter. We
were on the telephone for over an hour one evening last week,
and although at first, when he didn't have a clue who I was or
what I wanted, he was a little cautious – "thought you might
be wanting to sell me some double glazing or something like
that" – but once he understood the purpose of my call, he was
eager and willing to speak to me about Stephen, or as he put it
– "Our Bright Light In The North!"

Chapter Seventeen: Ghosts

Although many thousands of books have been written on the subjects of hauntings and ghosts no one has come up with a precise or definitive explanation of what exactly a ghost is. Theories vary from there being trace energies in the place of the haunting that cause some degree of time displacement when connected with the individual psyche of the person seeing the ghost or apparition, to the more controversial proposition of there being parallel worlds running on a different time scale of which we occasionally receive flash visions.

I suppose your belief in ghosts rather depends upon whether or not you've ever seen one, and to a lesser degree, how susceptible you might be in believing some of the stories that have been told and written. In this context, we are not talking about poltergeist activity (which has been very well researched and documented) and nor are we talking about atmospheric presences or hauntings in a purely psychological sense: what I *am* making reference to is Old Marley, The Headless Horseman, and the ubiquitous Grey Lady.

It is easy to dismiss the idea of ghosts until one has actually seen one – at which point in time one's subjective appreciation of the concept usually does a faster U turn than a politician in the The Houses Of Parliament!

Here I have a confession to make. In all of my years working within the realms of the paranormal, I have *never* seen a ghost! To be sure, I have sensed presences, some of them very strong indeed, and especially in the 1980's when I was exploring the avenues of Magick I was frequently aware of some extremely powerful forces moving around me – but never once have I come across headless horsemen or grey ladies and the like – although I have talked to any number of people who say that *they* have!

Stephen has, on one occasion, encountered a ghost, and it is interesting to note his reaction to it. The first thing that becomes glaringly apparent in Stephen's assessment of the phenomenon is the fact that the "ghost" was a totally different entity than a "spirit" and carried with it an entirely different energy.

When you are known as a spiritualist, or indeed as anyone who works within the fields of the paranormal, it's quite amazing how people will phone you up at all hours of the day wanting an instant fix to their problems. You become a lifeline and a crutch, and even though *you* might know that there isn't too much you can do for anyone over the 'phone other than to offer a few words of encouragement and advice, the message seldom sinks in with the person who is making the call. I had a client called Hank who used to phone me quite regularly from the United States, and always around tea-time. The trouble was that it was *his* tea-time, which for me was around two o'clock in the flaming morning! I'm sure that Hank was working for the CIA or some such organisation, (either that or he was a crook) and he'd always telephone just before some sort of operation – *Hy James, I'm just calling because I've got a very tricky job on tonight and I wondered if things were going to work out OK* – and even though he never paid me for it, I'd turn over a tarot card on the bedside table and suggest that (a) he either stayed at home or (b) that he had a good night out.

Stephen had an acquaintance called Paul who would frequently call him up when he was faced with a problem, and Stephen, being Stephen, would always do what he could to help. Paul was on thin ice though, when he called Stephen up at one o'clock in the morning, saying *"Steve, you've got to come round straight away because there's a ghost walking round my living room and its scaring me half to death!"*

As you can imagine, Stephen was not amused. He didn't exactly tell Paul to get lost, but he did make it clear that he had no intention of getting out of bed and driving half way across Wakefield in the middle of the night. Whatever the problem was, it could be sorted out in the morning.

Half an hour later the telelphone rang again and this time it was a young lady called Angela on the line. Angela was a mutual friend of both Stephen and Paul, and she was ringing to assure Stephen that Paul wasn't seeing things. That there really *was* a ghost wandering around Paul's living room, she too had seen it, and she really did think Stephen should come over, despite the lateness of the hour.

Much against his better judgement and against the protestations of Caroline who clearly thought he was off on a wild goose chase, Stephen climbed into a pair of jeans and a tea shirt, and drove bleary eyed to Paul's house on the other side of town.

Stephen: 'When I got there I could tell straight away that something was going on. Both Paul and Angela were agitated to say the least... Anyway, we went inside and had a cup of tea, and Paul and Angela both told me how they'd seen this figure of a little old man materialise in the middle of the room, before walking across the floor and disappearing through the wall. Neither of them had ever experienced anything like this before, and it had really got to them.

So anyway, we all sat together waiting for something to happen... I remember thinking that this was a load of old cobblers, and wondering how long I'd have to wait until I could make a reasonable excuse to get off home to my bed, and then, after about ten minutes, there it was... It was just standing there by the fire place, looking at the three of us, sprawled out on the settee. It was this little old man wearing nondescript and indistinct clothing that *might* have been Victorian... He simply stood there, silent but unmoving... No he wasn't the see-through sort of apparition you get in the movies, but neither was he wholly present either.

'I was out of my seat like a shot, almost as if a five ton mouse had just scurried across the room. I must have said something stupid like "what the hell is that?" or some such expression, and Angela said that it was their ghost. I think they were rather relieved at that moment – you know, to have their ghost confirmed by a third party, namely me, and I think that they were more than pleased that I could see it as well, because, of course, it meant that they were not having hallucinations or going off their trolleys.

'For my part, I didn't like it all. When I'm with a spirit, there's this lovely warm feeling of love suffusing all around me, and I feel incredibly safe and protected. But there was nothing like that here at all. It was a cold alien presence that made my hackles rise...

'Anyway, the figure walked in front of the fireplace and then did a right turn at the wall, and then walked over towards the other side of the room, and then when this little old character suddenly reached forward and grabbed at my leg I nearly jumped out of my skin. I can remember yelling "It's got my leg! It's got my leg!" – then just as quickly as it had materialised it disappeared. I never saw it again, and for that matter neither did Angela and Paul, but I have to confess that I did *not* like this experience! It wasn't nice at all – and whatever or whoever the little old man was, he wasn't a spirit in the mould of those spirits who come and talk to me when I'm giving a demonstration. And yet, here's the funny thing, I'm quite sure he knew I was there, and when he grabbed my leg, I actually felt his fingers wrap themselves around my knee. It wasn't anything that you'd call evil, just cold and alien and like I said before, not very nice. Even when I think about it now it gives me a fit of the shudders.'

'So, in retrospect, what do you make of this?' I ask.

'Hey,' says Stephen. 'You're the expert. You tell me.'

So what *are* we to make of all this? Despite Stephen's words I'm certainly not an expert on ghosts, although obviously I have had more than my fair share of paranormal experiences. Perhaps we need to detach ourselves from the subjective and look at some hard facts.

First of all, ghosts and their kin (hauntings and apparitions) have been recorded in the writings of all cultures since the beginning of history. One can take the scientific stance of this being hysteria and over active imagination, but one can just as easily say "there aint no smoke without fire", and surely not every ghostly sighting can be attributed to an unstable mind. Moreover some very *objective* minds made a point of studying in depth these phenomena in the 19th and 20th centuries, (everyone from Elifas Levi to our own Colin Wilson) and concluded that although the "ghost" was inexplicable it was none-the-less very real, even if only insofar as it was a real experience for the person encountering such an entity. We cannot see the wind but we know when it is blowing. We cannot explain the power of electricity but we know that it works.

Secondly, Stephen Holbrook had his first contact with a spirit when he was only thirteen years old. Since he was sixteen (almost seventeen years ago at the time of writing) he has had meaningful contact and dialogue with literally thousands of spirits who have proved the veracity and validity of their existence by the linking information which has been so very applicable and uniquely relevant to their loved ones left behind. Stephen is clairvoyantly and clairaudiently tuned to the world of spirit – in his own words *"I've got to sit down with a spirit right up in front of my eyes and have dinner with it before I'll believe it's really there"* – and if therefore he says that whatever it was that he encountered in his friend's home was something entirely different to what he understands to be a spirit – a warm, loving intelligent energy functioning with personality and individuality, albeit in a different dimension, then he more than anyone should be able to tell the difference and who can gainsay him?. I for one am prepared to take his words at their face value.

This incident seems to be of some specific relevance because it breaks with the long held tradition of belief that says there can be no interaction between Man and Ghost.

Indeed, as far as I know (lurid ghost stories apart) it is without precedent and it opens up a whole new strand of investigation.

Stephen not only *saw* the apparition in Paul's house, he also physically *felt* it when it grabbed at his leg. Of course one could put this down to Stephen's shock and to his imagination. Pardon the pun, but there is no doubt that he was 'spooked' by the incident, and in one sense it must be acknowledged that anyone who does what Stephen does for a living must have some heightened degree of imagination. But in another sense this argument falls apart, for it is through having faith in these very same qualities, the reality of his imagination and his powers of creative visualisation, that helps him to communicate with the spirit world in the first place!

What is obvious is that Paul and Angela's Little Old Man reacted to Stephen in a different way in which is reacted (or didn't react) to them, and the fact that it reacted at all makes one wonder whether it was a ghost in the accepted sense of the word. But, if not a ghost and if not a spirit, what else could it have been? …And of equal importance, where might it have come from?

Chapter Eighteen: Other Worlds

The mediaeval Church (and in certain quarters, the modern Church also, I suspect) had a very simple vision of other worlds. Basically, Heaven was "up", Hell was "down" and purgatory was vaguely somewhere in between. Science, of course, makes a mockery of this concept and although the modern Church readily accepts the science, it is maddeningly silent when it comes to presenting us with any kind of geographical location for these domains.

Various theories and convenient stratagems abound, the favourite being that Hell is our time spent down here on the Earthplane while Heaven is the spiritual plane of Grace to which we transcend after we die. Therefore, Heaven and Hell are not physical locations at all, but simply subjective states of mind.

In my own opinion these abstract concepts just won't do. They open the door to rampant speculation, answer none of the questions that demand answers, and indeed provoke many more questions that are impossible even to consider through lack of any basic terms of reference.

It is not too difficult to accept the principle of spiritual continuance of life after death, for without such a principle, enshrined in one form or another within the framework of all religions since the beginning of time, on an emotional level our lives would be even more filled with fear than they already are, and on a psychological level our lives would be rendered meaningless. What would be the point and purpose of life if, at the time of death all the lights went out, and that was it? Over! Finis! Kaput! Terminado! End of story!

Our egos and the essential cores of our personalities demand that life be worth more than this and we reach out to embrace the precedents set by nature to give our beliefs some substance and to allay our fears of the great unknown.

But there are some differences between humanity and nature. In nature flora regenerates, just as humankind regenerates through the process of procreation. This, however, is a purely *biological* process which makes no allowances for the sentient spiritual awareness of Man's identity which depends upon more than just physical procreation for its continued existence.

The crux of the question is – where do we go when we die? The abstract answer is that we go to Heaven, but for this answer to have any meaning at all, we must go on to ask where and what *is* Heaven? – And it is at this point that things start falling apart, for there are no proven answers!

For want of anything more tangible and concrete one can certainly pay some homage to the "Heaven is a state of mind" theory, and for my own part I am happy enough to accept that Heaven may well be what each individual needs and expects it to be on a purely subjective level. This theory is not without some precedent and common sense, for if nothing else it does provide a possible answer to *some* of the questions, giving weight to the idea that Heaven may well be a multi-layered space with many different dimensions. (*"In my Father's House there are many mansions!"*)

If your idea of Heaven is to be in a glorious shopping mall where all the items are free and you can shop 'till you drop, this is where you may well end up. Alternatively your vision of Heaven may be to dwell for eternity in a large football stadium where there is no charge for the beer – well, good luck to you! I find both visions equally appalling just as you might find *my* vision of Heaven – warm sunshine, turquoise blue seas, palm trees, white sand, fine wines and great poetry with Classic FM minus the dreadful adverts – equally abhorrent.

Therefore if we ask the most fundamental of questions – where does Stephen Holbrook get his messages from? – the answer may well be from all of these different stratas and spheres.

On a number of occasions I have broached this subject with Stephen and his answer has always been the same.

146

'Look, I've read a load of books written by other clairvoyants and mediums where they've claimed to have had visions of Heaven, sometimes describing it as a beautiful garden with endless views of flowers and plants, sometimes seeing it as a place of perpetual summer where the skies are always blue and the fields are gentle meadows of verdant green... It's usually full of tame animals and there's inevitably a meandering river full of friendly fish or a babbling brook full of spring clear water fresh enough to drink...

'But for the life of me I don't know where they get their information from. I've been working closely with spirit for more than seventeen years and although it may be a disappointment to some people, all I can say is I've never had any visions of anything like that.

'You ask me where the messages come from, and I can only explain it as another dimension of spiritual existence. I don't know where it is or what it is – but I do feel that it is very close to us, neither above nor below, but all around. I know that when a spirit is communicating through me, it's right there next to me, standing by my elbow and speaking in my ear.

'There are some other things that I am fairly sure about. For example, animals have spirits and souls just like us, and just like us, they enjoy a life after death. I know this to be true on the strength of the number of times an animal has come through as part of the link. It can be a dog or a cat, a horse or a canary. There are no reservations. Also, despite what the Church used to say, I know that suicides transcend to this higher sphere of spiritual existence just like everybody else. I get quite a number of suicides coming through; they're always particularly strong links and they always seem to try that bit harder to get their messages across.'

The Bible, The Church and Hammer Horror Films have one thing in common, which is their belief that evil spirits are abroad in this world. While Stephen does not dismiss the concept out of hand, he is quite clear in his own mind that he has never met or had any dealings with one.

'There are,' he says, 'some very evil *people* but I don't think there are any evil spirits. I've never met one, anyway. An evil person dies and they take their evil with them to the other side. I don't know what happens exactly, and to tell you the truth I don't think anyone else knows for sure either, but what I *think* happens is that the evil is exorcised by a process of checks and balances. In a spiritual sense we atone for the misdeeds we have committed while down here on the Earthplane. I think there is some sort of process whereby we work a lot of spiritual overtime, but how long that takes, the Lord only knows, because the way I sense it, time on the spiritual plane runs very differently to the way it does down here on planet Earth.

'And there's something else that seems to get sorted out once we've crossed over to the other side. If you've been mangled in a bad car crash, you're unmangled. If your body has wasted away with some dreadful disease like cancer, then in spirit you are made whole again. Paradoxically though, you still retain your personality... If you were a jolly cheerful soul down here, you'll be a jolly cheerful soul over there. If you were a grumpy old codger, you're likely to remain a grumpy old codger... Having said that, all the anger and hatred is removed, all the hang-ups, and where it exists, all the evil.'

I have to say that I am not sure I entirely agree with Stephen on the subject of evil spirits, but I am completely in sympathy with what he has to say about the process of spiritual healing and the ambiguity of time – for this moves us into other spheres of other-worldliness.

In occult philosophy the concept of other worlds is a familiar one, and just to put your mind at rest, let us first deal with this mischievous word "occult". Again I refer to my trusty old dictionary, and I quote: *"Involving the supernatural, mystical, magical; that which is kept secret or hidden, esoteric, recondite, mysterious, not obvious on inspection:* occultist – *he or she who works with the mysteries and seeks that which is hidden; the seeker of hidden truth, he or she who strives to master arcane knowledge."* – Please note, not a word here about witches, hobgoblins, Satanists or any kind of sexual depravation. Indeed, by definition, a research scientist is an occultist, as is any kind of theologian who is taking his or her work seriously rather than spouting cant. As you can see, our friends at Hammer Horror have a lot to answer for, along with people like Dennis Wheatly, Dean Koontz, James Herbert and Steven King!

I am not being disingenuous here and I am well aware of the fact that certain base and negative energies have tried to shanghaiy occultism by bending the meaning of the word to fit their own criteria and to justify their own reasons for existence, but in its pure form that word 'occult' is both innocuous and demanding, depending upon how you choose to interpret it. Suffice to say that occult thought embraces the concept of the following planes of existence.

First there is the Earthplane where we live on a conscious level. One level above that there is Dreamworld to which our subconscious minds, both independently and collectively, escape while we are sleeping. One (very ill-defined) level above that there is The Astral Plane, which occasionally we visit in our dreamstate, but which is a different sphere of consciousness altogether: elements of thought and energy alien to our dreams also exist on this plane which filter "up" from our subconscious and "down" from the plane above, which is defined as being The First Spiritual Plane – a zone which is *inhabited?* – by our "higher" spiritual selves and the "lower" Angelic energies of the plane above that. Therefore, on The Astral Plane there are a great many psycho-dramatic conflicts between our lower and our higher instincts: the base energy of Man confronts the Angelic energy of The Godhead, and there

149

is dichotomy and disarray. It is only when we transcend The Astral Plane and enter The First Spiritual Plane that we arrive in the place of True Spirit. While The Dreamer and The Occultist can access The Astral Plane, neither can access the plane above – but at the point of death we are immediately catapulted beyond The Dreamstate and The Astral into The First Spiritual Plane where we confront (a) our own Higher Spiritual Selves and (b) the key Angelic energies that have governed our lives and have defined our characters and personalities, not to mention our actions and our attitudes, our successes and our failures.

Upon this First Spiritual Plane we are *very* close to our old human lives and our loved ones left behind, and it is esoteric philosophy which suggests that it is from *this* sphere that the clairvoyant or medium will make contact with the spirits of the departed: this is the domain of unfinished business, the staging post between Earthplane existence and transcendence to other worlds of consciousness that bring the individual ever closer to the totality of pure spiritual integration with his or her higher self and the energy or entity that gave it life in the first instance.

Beyond this First Spiritual Plane there are other levels of spiritual purity to which the spirit graduates as and when it chooses to, or indeed, as and when it can! Promotion within the realms of the Spiritual Hierarchy is awarded on merit not seniority, and to acquire that merit, a spirit must evolve and develop. Thus, service, be it in the form of spiritual guidance or in the form of reincarnational input to the greater good of the world, becomes inevitable within this concept of duty and spiritual responsibility.

If we are asked to consider the size of the universe, or how many light years it is to Alpha Centauri, or just how big was The Big Bang, then our minds move into overload: mathematicians might revel in the mystery of their numerical equations, but as for the rest of us, we simply cannot grasp the concepts that are being presented to us. And so, I suspect, it is with those other concepts of planes of Spiritual Existence which transcend the First Spiritual Plane; in short, we haven't a clue what we're talking about, we don't even know exactly what we think, and when we *do* try to wrap our minds around the concept our senses disintegrate into a melange of incomprehension.

However, that First Spiritual Plane is *just* within reach of our understanding, and it is that plane and the planes *below* it that need further consideration at this point.

None of us likes to leave unfinished business.   None of us likes to leave without saying goodbye. All of us care about the welfare and well-being of those we love and hold dear to our hearts. These are basic human qualities, and even if you were the most base of human beings, i.e. Adolf Hitler, then history records that Hitler was dotingly dedicated equally to his mistress (Eva Braun) and to their much loved and adored Alsatian dogs.

Is it then not both natural and inevitable that before transcending into some more distant realm of spiritual purity, the spirit of someone departed from this Earthplane realm of existence might want to say goodbye to a loved one, might want to bring some succour and comfort, some semblance of support and reassurance to someone in need? Might they not also want to reassure their loved ones left behind that there *is* an afterlife, and because of that guarantee, offered not by some slick salesperson but by someone known, loved and trusted, there need be no fear of death?   And is it not reasonable to believe that life, once the fear of death has been removed, does not become more rewarding, more meaningful, more enjoyable? Surely, if there is no fear of death, the living can get on with the business of living, and make that life (whether you are a millionaire superstar or confined within the mobile cage of a wheelchair) really count for something splendid within the framework of human experience?

151

I can remember, many many years ago, sitting in the beer garden of a lovely old English pub at Marlow Bottom. It was a glorious autumn day, warm, bright and sunny, more of an Indian summer than an Autumnal Sunday. I had a friend with me... She was young, no more than eighteen (well it *was* a long time ago) and she was very talented and very beautiful. On this particular day she was very quiet and moody, and a cloud of negativity hung over her like a wet blanket. Fearing that I had said or done something to upset her, I asked her what was wrong... And what she said appals me just as much now as it did then. Basically, she told me that she was scared stiff of dying. Yes, she knew that she was young and healthy, but she was also aware of the fact that this would not (could not) always be the case, and that sometime along the pathway of her future she would (just like the rest of us) have to face death. This thought chilled her to the bone, and she saw no point in living if no matter what she did with her life, she was destined to die. Might as well die now rather than wait for Death to come sneaking up on her in her old age... And besides, what was the point of living, *what was the point of planning anything in life* if she could suddenly get knocked down by a bus, or struck by lightening or if there was a nuclear war?

I wonder how she might have felt or how much her life might have been changed had Stephen Holbrook been there to provide her with a message of love from her Grandmother or her Grandfather, bringing through some hard evidence that Death is but a portal from one world to another?

Although Stephen himself cannot qualify or quantify his own talent, I feel sure that he brings messages through from spirits who dwell on that First Spiritual Plane of existence, spirits who not only need to, but want to offer messages of hope and comfort to those folk they have left behind. When he is working on the platform he is in direct contact with spiritual identities who lower themselves through the murk of The

Astral (quite a painful and laborious process, and probably quite a weakening one as well) to make contact: those who cannot endure the lowering of their vibration may well shout across the divide, which explains why some messages (a very few) and unclear and indistinct.

With reference to The Little Old Man in Paul's Victorian terraced house, we now have the glimmering of an explanation. Not a spirit, for there was no love and warmth. Not a ghost, for there was physical interaction. Not an evil spirit, for Stephen would be the first to admit there was no 'evil' energy present... And therefore the logical conclusion is something manifest or picked up from The Astral, where dreamstate visions and subconscious elements all too easily impress themselves upon the open minds of the unwary, especially if, as in this case, the unwary also happened to be clairvoyantly tuned in to the presence of other world dimensions.

As a footnote to this long and complicated chapter I feel impelled to add a personal note of evidence on the subject of an after death process of spiritual healing. My Grandmother died when she was a crumpled old lady of 94, but on the few occasions when she has made her spiritual presence felt, either in my dreams or at the psychic table, she has presented herself as a very sprightly sixty year old.

A few years ago, a very special friend died of multiple cancer, and in the last six months of his life he dropped from twelve stones to six and a half stones – and yet when he has visited me, again in that kind of dream which for me is always more than just a dream, not only has he been his hail and hearty old self, he has also smartened up his appearance: in life he was content to slouch around in old pants and scruffy tea-shirts, but in the afterlife he seems more at home in smart flannels, natty blazers and club ties.

A short while after Garth Odell passed over another friend was killed on Spain's notorious N340, and without going into details, Sam was in a physical mess before he lost his fight for life. And yet when Sam comes through to me in my dreams and waking visions, he's still the Sam that I knew and loved, full of life and laughter with not so much as a shaving cut or bruise.

Like Stephen I am not evangelical. This is my experience and evidence. I believe it and accept it... and you must find your own!

Stephen – on Stephen and Everyday Life

I love gardening! It's the only thing that relaxes me completely! If you take a typical week in my life – well, I get up on a Monday morning with Caroline and the kids and help get the kids ready for school. It's chaos! Bradley is running round at my heels pulling at my trousers while Robbie, who's six in June, tries to eat cocoa pops while he's watching the TV, and then five minutes before it's time to leave the house he's got to wash his face, comb his hair and get all his stuff ready for school... While all this is happening the mobile is ringing like mad with people wanting to make bookings for the various shows and Caroline is trying to get Ellie, our youngest, ready for her day... Then when it's time for me to take Robbie to school Bradley causes a fuss because he wants to come with us, and of course, he can't...

I drive Robbie to school then drive back home and make a start on all the work that needs doing, arranging the advertising for the demonstrations, checking that the press releases have all gone out for the following two or three weeks... It's an intense two or three hours, and then I have to go back into town to bank the takings from the business. I might take half an hour out to mooch around the second hand shops because I love getting a bargain and I actually like buying a lot of my gear from the charity shops. The charity shops are worth spending money with. I'll often buy something for ten or fifteen quid and from the reaction I get I know I've made somebody's day!

Then its back home again and another couple of hours on the 'phone – I'll get a bite of lunch then escape to the garden to unwind, watering, chopping, weeding, and when it's time to go and collect Robbie I'm feeling a bit more human... Bradley will have been with me all day and that's okay because I think that parents and fathers in particular should make more time to be with their children, which is one of the reasons why I like to take the boys swimming at least twice a week... So much time is taken up with work and I seldom get chance to put the kids to bed at night because I'm out on the road, so I like to compensate for this whenever and however I can.

After swimming I'll spend half an hour getting myself ready then its into the car and out onto the motorway – could be Retford, could be Durham, could be Chester – I'll do the dem then drive back, and probably won't be home much before midnight. Then I'll have some tea, which is a terrible time to eat but I hate eating before a show because of the nerves: I have to feel empty before I go on stage otherwise I don't function properly...

Even though I'm always shattered, I manage to unwind on the drive home. This is my thinking time and I go over the evening in my mind, wondering how effective I was and being amazed and thankful for the evidence I've been able to bring through.

Tuesday will be a repeat of Monday but on Wednesday I'm back at work in the salon – that's anything between fifteen and twenty clients per day, fifteen to twenty half hour conversations, and all the time the phone is ringing, either Caroline or Roger Prior from Devon, or it could be you phoning from York or any one of a dozen other people all who want to talk to me for some reason or another. Nine times out of ten all I can do is take a message and promise to call people back as soon as I'm free...

Thursday and Friday are a repeat of Wednesday and without doubt Saturday is my busiest day. By the time I get to Sunday I just want to collapse, but I'm usually demonstrating somewhere on Sunday night, and Sunday is also the only time I really get to be the family man I want to be. We don't always do anything exciting on a Sunday, but that's okay as long as we can all be together as a family for a while.

My working life never seems to stop, and as soon as I'm at home I'm a father again... Daddy come and look at this, or Daddy Daddy come and do the other with me, or Daddy come and tell me a story... It's lovely but I'm exhausted, and as soon as my head hits the pillow, I've gone. Believe me, I don't have any trouble sleeping!

Then on top of all this there's the charity work that I do for the Spiritualist Church: I do regular stints for Chairrobics in Bradford and Una Pearce's Candlelighters for the children's' hospice in Huddersfield. Then, of course, I do frequent demonstrations on behalf of Breast Cancer and LAD at the Royal Marsden Hospital, oh, and there's the Bud Flanagan Leukaemia Appeal... I do so many, and these are just a few... I feel good about doing them because you bring people into the venues that probably wouldn't come under normal circumstances: they come because they're supporting a good cause but it still gives me the opportunity to make them think about life after death and to take away some of the fear. On average, I work about a hundred hours a week but it's worth it. I've got to believe that or I simply couldn't do it!

I'm very lucky because I get a fantastic amount of support from my family and my friends. My Mum was very unsure in the early days, but now she's thrilled to bits and my Dad, who is not the best person in the world when it comes to showing his emotions, probably because of the era of his upbringing, is very proud of me and he follows me around everywhere. It wasn't always that way though, and I remember it did take him five years to come and see one of my demonstrations. I've got two gorgeous sisters in Adel and Joanne and they've always been behind me one hundred percent of the way and I'm glad that my mediumship has been able to help them from time to time over the years...

...And I can't tell you how much I value my friends! People like Una Pearce and Janet Fergussen and Jane

McDonald... The people who were with me right from the beginning! And other friends like Roger and Gill Prior who have done so much for me in the West Country... Roger and Gill have never actually had a message from me, but they've seen me work, and I've helped them to believe in spiritualism, which in turn has done something to help them deal with the enormity of their tragedy... They lost their daughter when she was only twenty three years old, but through visiting the spiritualist church, they have had lots of hard evidence to prove that there is an afterlife and that their lovely Lisa is alive and well, dancing on rainbows on the other side of the veil...

Chapter Nineteen: A Wynter's Tale

Rather perversely in her own estimation of the event, Avril Wynter was born in the Mid-summer – June 29th 1968. The place of her birth was Noctorum on The Wirral and she spent the first ten years of her life growing up within a perfect example of the family ideal. Her parents, George and Megan Wynter, were financially successful in their respective fields of banking and journalism, which gave Avril and her dotingly protective brother Michael (older by three years) a comfortable if not exactly privileged childhood.

'I think,' she says, 'that these were without doubt the happiest days of my life. I have wonderful memories of long summer holidays, sailing our old boat up and down the River Dee, of Mike teaching me how to fish and how to ride a bike, of travelling to France and living in this old farmhouse for half a year while Mummy tried to write a novel. We were an incredibly close family and Mike and I were not just brother and sister, we were also best friends. We both loved our parents, and for their part, our parents adored us both. They brought us up sensibly, taught us some proper values, but there was never a sense of heavy handed discipline. I don't remember crying much, but I do remember laughing an awful lot.'

This idyllic existence came to an abrupt end on May 21st 1978 when Michael Wynter was killed in a boating accident. He had been sailing in the estuary with two friends, and either through a freak pattern of winds and tides, or possibly because the three boys had been "larking about" and had not been paying sufficient attention to what they should have been doing, their dinghy had capsized half a mile off shore. All three young lives were lost.

'It was as though someone had drawn a black veil over our lives,' Avril remembers. 'All three of us went into a state of deep shock and mourning, and we all felt Michael's loss in our different ways. I suppose it was particularly difficult for me. I was only ten years old, and could not understand what had happened or why it had happened. Mummy and Daddy did their best for me, but they were so cut up themselves that they really couldn't get into my head and explain things properly. Maybe they couldn't explain it because they just didn't know how.

'After Michael died we all tried to carry on as normal but it didn't work. I mean, how *could* it work? Anyway, we all struggled on for the next couple of years. We went on holiday to Spain and did the usual things that families do at Christmas and Easter, but it seemed that we were just going through the motions. The lights were on but nobody was home.

'Daddy followed the old masculine cliché of throwing himself into his work and I suppose, on thinking back, that I must have realised something wasn't quite right. He seemed to spend more and more time away from home and my Mother and I started doing more things on *our* own. If Mummy knew things that I didn't know, obviously she didn't tell me about them, but it all came to a head when Daddy went missing for a weekend, and the police finally found him in his car with a hose pipe from the exhaust shoved through the back window...

'There wasn't a suicide note or anything like that, but it came out at the inquest that Daddy had been seeing the doctor for depression and that he had been under incredible pressure at work.

'I was twelve when this happened and I just curled up inside myself. I couldn't tell anyone how I felt – I didn't *know* how I felt or even how I was *supposed* to feel – in fact, when I think back to that time, maybe I didn't feel anything at all. I was just numb from head to toe.

'Mummy was in pretty well the same state, and of course, what we should have done was talk to each other... We should have tried to find some mutual support in each other's love, but it didn't happen like that. I locked myself into my own little world, and she locked herself in her's.'

In the late summer of 1981 Megan Wynter sold the old family home on The Wirral and moved herself and her daughter to Provence in the South of France. With the sale of the house and the insurances from her husband's death there was (at that time) no shortage of money, and for the following six years, Megan went through the process of spending it – initially on buying a home near Avion, on subsidising herself while she tried to write a book, and on putting Avril through one of the best private schools in the district, but as Megan's lifestyle became increasingly bohemian, so her choice of company became increasingly questionable, and her consumption of alcohol just increased, full stop.

Avril: 'I would come back to the house after school and could find any one of half a dozen people hanging out, just about every drop-out and hanger on in the community, drinking Mummy's booze and smoking dope or whatever. I know she was having regular sex with at least three different guys, and I hated it – and I hated it even more when I started to get some of that kind of attention. By the time I was sixteen I was a long leggy blond, and I had my own friends, and my own boyfriend, which was okay, and I was happy with that, but every time I was with Mummy's crowd I could feel these older male eyes ogling me and I never knew when someone was going to make a grab at me. Mummy and I weren't close by that time, in fact we were fighting like cat and dog, and in my deepest heart of hearts, I just wanted to leave and get out, which I did, but not for another couple of years.'

On the evening of Avril's 18th birthday she was celebrating with a few friends in one of the local village bars. She had packed an overnight bag and had fully intended staying with her boyfriend and his sister, full well knowing that Megan was having "a few of her own friends round for the night."

At a little before midnight Avril's birthday party came to an abrupt halt when a police car arrived at the local bar and three officers, two male, one female, took Avril away to identify her Mother's body in the morgue. There had been an argument and a fight, Megan Wynter had been stabbed to death, and a local man was being held in custody.

Avril: 'I wish I could say that I felt a great sense of grief, but I honestly can't. Once the initial shock had worn off I felt deeply sad – sad for what my Mother and I had once been to each other, and sad for what she had become and how she had died. But I also felt a profound sense of relief – and an awful lot of guilt about feeling relieved! I suppose on a psychological level I closed down even more... Mike had gone, then Daddy, and now Mummy as well – none of them in normal or natural circumstances, and I began to feel that everything I touched or loved was doomed to come to a terrible end.

'Mummy had used up all the money, so all I got was what the sale of the house in Provence brought in – I was eighteen years old, had no family left at all, and although I *did* have friends in Provence, they weren't really what you'd call close friends: I was sort of half in love with this boy called Paulus, we'd been sleeping together for about eighteen months, but it wasn't really going anywhere, so once the money was in my bank account I just packed my bags and left.'

Avril first went to Paris where she worked for three years as an interpreter for an Anglo-French oil company, and from there she went to Tunisia, this time working as a translator for another oil company. She says: 'I'm not proud of it, but I was attractive and had dozens of lovers during that five year period. None of them lasted more than a few months and the moment anyone started getting too close or looked for any kind of commitment, that was it – I was out of it and gone like a shot from a gun. I simply knew that I couldn't afford to love anyone or anything again, because the moment I did, that would be taken from me as well.'

162

In 1991 two things occurred to change Avril's life completely. The first was that she was taken seriously ill with food poisoning which then developed into something more serious: although never coming anywhere close to death, she was none the less very poorly and for a number of weeks was confined to a hospital ward in Hammamet. It was here that she met a young English doctor called Kevin Waldron, and despite herself, she found herself falling seriously in love with this gentleman – just as he fell head over heels in love with her. Despite numerous proposals of marriage, she steadfastly refused – but a strong relationship *did* develop and when Kevin returned to the UK in 1992, Avril returned with him.

'First of all we lived in London and then moved on to Cambridge, and we were really very happy. Kevin had his work and I had mine, we lived our separate lives, but we lived them together. The only thing that ever caused a dark cloud was Kevin's desire for me to walk down the aisle with him; it did cause some friction, but we worked round it, and although it did cause a problem now and again, it wasn't a huge problem – or at least, I didn't think it was until we had this dreadful fight, believe it or not, on my birthday, the 29th of June 1995. All that happened was I got a phone call from an old boyfriend in Tunisia, just to say hello, how was I, and to wish me a happy birthday. Anyway, Kevin got very jealous and angry, and before we knew it we were in a full scale row. It ended up with him saying that if I didn't love him enough to marry him, I didn't love him enough full stop, and if that was the case it was high time he started looking for someone else who did! I was as cross as he was, and rather stupidly told him that I thought that was a very good idea. The next day he packed his things and left, and that was it – five years down the pan, just like that!'

It took Avril a few weeks to realise that the relationship was in fact over, and while her pride and natural self defence mechanisms made it impossible for her to try and correct the situation, she was none-the-less acutely depressed and unhappy.

At this point some element of instinct took over. 'I realised that the only place I had ever been happy in my life was on The Wirral, on the banks of the River Dee, so that's where I moved back to, in search of my lost childhood. I bought a small cottage half a mile from our old family home, and spent the next years doing freelance translation work for anyone who needed my services. I tried to write a book and had no better luck than my Mother, and I tried writing poetry, some of which did get published, but it wasn't very good. I kept myself to myself, became something of a recluse really, and got used to my own company.

'I did make one friend – a lady called Maggie who lived near Birkenhead and who I used to have coffee with at the local poetry group meetings – she took me under her wing, and it was Maggie who told me that a clairvoyant medium was coming to Liverpool and wanted to know if I'd go with her to see him. This was March of this year (2000) and although I really didn't know anything about mediumship or believe in life after death, I thought I might as well go just to see what it was all about, and, of course, to keep Maggie company.

'I wasn't sure quite what to expect, but I was certainly impressed by Mr Holbrook's sincerity and passion, and Maggie was absolutely delighted because she got a message from her daughter who had died when she was still a little girl of seven or eight years old. Stephen Holbrook said he wanted to talk to someone on our row who had lost a daughter while she was still only quite little, and that he was getting a strong link with the letter M... Well that was Maggie's initial, of course, but it was also the initial of her daughter's name as well – Maggie's daughter was called Maudie. So Maggie put her hand up and Stephen then told her lots of things about her daughter's life that nobody else could possibly have known about, even down to the way that Maudie had cried her heart out when her pet hamster had died...

'As I say, Maggie was very impressed, and it made me very thoughtful for a few weeks. In fact, to tell you the truth, I couldn't get the man's face out of my mind, and I kept asking myself over and over again how he could have known the things that he knew, and not just about Maggie's daughter but about all of those other people in the room that he gave messages to.

'In the end, I phoned the Moat House Hotel in Liverpool and asked when Mr Holbrook would be returning, and they gave me a date in October. I mulled that over for a couple of days, then 'phoned the number on the little poster I'd been given, and talked to a very nice lady who told me that the nearest Stephen was going to be to Liverpool was Bolton on the 30th of April.

'Right up until the last minute I wasn't sure whether I was going to go or not, but I was restless all day and there wasn't anything much good on the television, and Bolton is less than an hour from where I live, so in the end I just jumped into the car and off I went.

'I went to Bolton out of curiosity, not really expecting to get a message, just wanting to know more about what Stephen could do and how he did it, but I did get a message – and you know the rest!'

I smiled over the rim of my coffee cup. 'Yes Avril *I* know what happened next, but the readers of this book don't, so just tell them in your own words.'

'Well, as I say, I wasn't expecting a message. I sat on the back row, looking a bit scruffy compared with everyone else in the room, and huddled down in my chair to watch what went on. Stephen talked to a lot of different people and I remember feeling a bit frustrated because although I could hear everything that Stephen said, I couldn't always catch the answers and reactions of the people he was talking to. And then he was looking down the whole length of the room and asking if there was anyone at the back who could understand a winter birthday and the number 29. He repeated this two or three times, and then said that the person he wanted to talk to would have a very important anniversary towards the end of June. I mean, I knew straight away it was for me, winter and my name Wynter, and my birthday being on the 29th of June, but I just couldn't get my mouth to open and I stayed quiet hoping that he would pass on to somebody else. He wasn't having any of that though and said that he wasn't going to leave this alone until he'd made contact with the right person because there was somebody called Michael waiting to say hello...

'I suppose it was Mike's name that jolted me into action, and without really realising that I was doing it, I was putting my hand up in the air and saying "hello, over here!"'

'He asked me if I could understand the significance of the number 29, and I told him yes I could, and then he said that there were two anniversaries associated with this number, both a birth and a death, and could I just say yes or no to that – so of course I had to tell him yes. Then he asked me if I could connect the number 29 to the month of June, and again I told him yes. Then he asked me outright if that was my birthday, so again I had to say yes, and then he said that the person who had died on that date, and it would have been quite a few years ago, had loved me very very much, but that she had had so many problems in her own life that she'd just forgotten how to show it. He said that he had a lady on the stage with him who had died very violently and that it hadn't been an accident! He said he knew that there was someone called Michael very close to me in spirit, and that Michael was giving him another big letter M as the initial of the lady who had been killed, and did this make any sense?

'Obviously it made all the sense in the world, so again I was able to say yes. Then he went on to say that the lady who

166

had passed over had died in another country, not in England, that she had been very unhappy in the latter years of her life, and that now, from the other side, she was so sorry that she had made me so unhappy... At that point I started to cry, and oh Lord I'm doing it again now... Can you turn that tape recorder off for a minute?'

I turn off the tape. Avril goes to the ladies room, and five minutes later we resume.

'To say that I was both moved and amazed by what Stephen was saying to me about my Mother is a major understatement of the truth. But it didn't end there. I mean, he actually asked me who Megan was, and I told him that it was my Mother's name... And then he asked me if I could understand the name of George, that this George would also have died quite a number of years ago, and that there would be some kind of link with a car. I told him yes, and wanted to tell him more, but you know what he's like, he only lets you answer yes or no. Then he wanted to know if I could understand what he meant if he told me that George's death wasn't an accident, but the way he died had something to do with the car he'd just spoken of... So again I said yes, and Stephen went on to tell me that George had been very confused and very unhappy, that he'd been very depressed, and hadn't really known what he was doing, and that it was only when he'd got over to the other side that he'd realised what an enormous mistake he'd made. Stephen told me that George was sending me all his love, and then Stephen wanted me to know that George had a very strong link, either with banking or accountancy, and that he was telling me that I should attempt to make my emotional life as strong as my financial life. Then Stephen said something which was so specific... He said "your Daddy wants you to know that he didn't feel any pain when he fell asleep in the car, but he did feel the pain when he woke up in Heaven and realised that he'd left you behind without even saying goodbye." He also wanted me to know that he was with Mummy again, and that

Michael was with them as well, and they all loved me very very much. They knew that my life hadn't been calm or happy, but they promised that things would start getting a little better, now that this contact had been made.

'Stephen then went on to talk about Michael, first of all asking me if I could remember there being a boating accident when I was still a little girl...

'Again, I told him yes... I mean I'll remember the day that Mike died till the day I die myself. Stephen said that three people had died in the accident, and that one of them was called Michael, and then he asked me if Michael was my brother. After I'd confirmed this Stephen said that the accident had occurred not at sea or on a lake but on a very wide river, and that the name of the river might begin with the letter D... This is where I broke Stephen's "just yes or no rule" and told him that it had been the River Dee. Then Stephen said that he had a message from Michael and that the message was "that it wasn't his fault!" Then Stephen told me that I'd done a lot of travelling in the past, he mentioned France and North Africa and Ireland, but that I'd been stuck in a rut for quite a while, and that soon it would be time to move on... Then he wanted to know if I could link with anyone called Fred or Freddy who had died of a fall within the last three months, and I couldn't, but the lady three rows directly in front of me could, and that's when Stephen said good night and God bless to me and was just about to move on to this other lady, when he paused and came back to me and asked "Why do I see you surrounded by snow and ice? Why is there this picture of winter all around you...?" And I told him, which was something that made the rest of the audience laugh for some reason, and then he went on to talk to the other lady about this chap called Freddy... And that's my story really, except for one funny little thing that happened last week...

'Stephen had mentioned Ireland, which made no sense to me at all whatsoever, but then out of the blue I had a post-card last Tuesday from Dublin. It was from Kevin, although Lord knows what prompted him to write to me – I mean I haven't heard a word from him for more than two years. It was just to say hello and that he was living and working in Dublin and that he hoped I was okay. He put a 'phone number on the card in case I felt like ringing him up for a chat.'

'And will you?' I ask

Avril smiles. 'It's a nice thought, isn't it? – But no, I probably won't. I don't think you can ever go backwards and Kevin would definitely be a backwards step. But it is odd that less than a fortnight after Stephen mentioned Ireland this post-card should arrive on my mat.'

'How do you feel now about the messages Stephen brought through for you? I mean, I don't want to put words in your mouth, but would you say that your experience has changed your life?

'No,' Avril replies promptly, 'my life is just the same, but what *has* changed is how I think and feel about my life. My life is the same, but I am different, and I'm still trying to work out the nuances.'

I thank her for taking the time to meet me and to tell me her story.

'Oh you're welcome... When I heard you were writing this book I thought you might like to know what it's like to be on the receiving end of the kind of evidence Stephen brings through, and the other thing is, it's so frustrating just saying yes or no, and I just thought Stephen himself might like to know just how accurate and specific he is with his messages.'

I thank Avril Wynter one more time, and then turn off the tape recorder.

Chapter Twenty: Testimony

In this day and age when we are far more inclined to write letters of complaint than we are to send letters of praise, it is both humbling and reassuring to read the many letters that have arrived on my desk since this book project began. All of these letters (and in many cases 'phone calls) have been unsolicited and have come from people who have heard about "The Light In The Darkness" and who have wanted to share their experiences with me. In every instance the people who have made contact tell me that their lives or the way in which they look at their lives have been changed through their contact with Stephen, and where and when they have found their way into this book I have used their real names and identities (bar one – the case of the gentleman from Retford – whose anonymity I have protected for obvious reasons.)

Again and again a common theme runs through this growing file of testimony – that it is the little things Stephen comes out with – that lends such great weight to the evidence of post mortem survival.

Gwen from Goole: "Stephen brought a message through from my late husband. He mentioned that Malcom had gone over with pains in the chest, which was obviously true because Mal did die of a heart attack. Stephen also got the date right when he said it was in the August, either the 17th or the 18th (it was actually the 17th) and when he said it would have been within the last twenty four months, he was right about that too, because it was almost two years to the week. But the thing that really impressed me was the fact that Mal had this fantastic way with birds, and for the last year of his life he actually had a tame jackdaw for a pet. He'd found it lying in a field with a broken wing, and he'd brought it home and patched it up, and ever since then Mal and that jackdaw were inseparable. Wherever Mal went, the jackdaw went too, and when we were at home watching the telly, the bird would sit on Mal's shoulder, just like a parrot. Anyway, Stephen said that Mal had got this bird with him, sitting on his shoulder, and that it wasn't a parrot, or a budgie or anything like that, and that it was actually a jackdaw...'

Cyril from Chester: 'I saw Stephen Holbrook on three separate occasions before I actually got a message, and when I did get a message, I was absolutely amazed. I haven't got any family, and even as a lad, I didn't have many people around me, but there was my brother Ned who got killed in the last days of the Second World War. Stephen told me that Ned had popped in to say hello, told me that he'd been a soldier killed in action, at least forty years ago, and that Ned's message was that he could still roll a fag with one hand. Even when we were youngsters Ned was ever so proud of this little trick and it was the one sure thing Stephen could have told me to prove that Ned was really there...'

Mandy from Otley: 'My boyfriend Nigel was killed on his motor bike six weeks before Christmas and to cap it all, it actually happened on his birthday, November the 19th. Christmas was awful and I had a very hard time coming to terms with what had happened. Anyway, the message that I got from Stephen was that someone with the initial letter N had been killed on his birthday a few weeks before the Christmas break, that the number 19 was very significant, that Nigel was was okay and that he loved me very much... That he was very sorry that he'd spoiled everybody's Christmas but that it wasn't his fault... Stephen also said that the motor bike had been a Kawasaki (which was right) and he also spoke of the St. Christopher medallion that Nigel had been wearing, which had been a birthday present I'd given him the year before and which he never took off his neck. He also was right about the fact that I dropped the St. Christopher into Nigel's coffin just before they closed the lid...'

Christine from Durham: 'I married John when I was still only seventeen. We'd been married for more than twenty years, and when he died of a brain tumour back in 1996 my

171

whole world ended. I tried to get a message from John for years and had seen loads of different clairvoyants, but nothing ever came through. Then this friend told me about Stephen Holbrook, and although I didn't have much hope, I went along for the evening, you know, just a "one last chance" sort of thing. Anyway Stephen came to me straight away, and told me that he had a link with someone called John who had passed over within the last five years, that this person had been progressively ill for the last twelve months of his life, and that the cause of the illness was "something wrong with his head." He mentioned the names of James and Joshua (our two sons) and said that John was looking after all three of us from the other side. He also mentioned the town of Morpeth which was where we'd been living when John had died, and said that the dates 18th of May and 4th of September were very important as anniversaries, which they were because May 18th was our wedding anniversary and John's funeral was held on the 4th of September. Stephen also said he was getting the strong impression of a pair of old cowboy boots, and did this mean anything to me? – It most certainly did because John had bought this pair of boots when we were on holiday in California back in 1992 and ever after he virtually lived in them, and it became an ongoing family joke...'

Norman from York: 'Our son Tony was killed on active service in Northern Ireland back in 1986 – an IRA bomb, and although the army took care of everything, there can't have been much left of him to bury. Apart from the army the one great love in Tony's life was Elvis Presley. He'd got every record Elvis had ever made and had a room full of posters and magazine articles, two or three autographs, and even one of Elvis's stage shirts that he'd got at an auction for a ridiculous amount of money. We hung onto all this stuff for years then I was made redundant and we became very strapped for cash. Something had to go, and with much regret and an awful lot of guilt, we sold all of the Elvis stuff, and it brought in just enough money to tide us over – but as I say, we felt very

172

guilty about it. When we went to see Stephen Holbrook at The Guildhall, he said he had a message from someone who had died in a massive explosion, and that the name of Tony or Tommy would be very important, and that there was a link with both Ireland and the USA. My wife and I both put our hands up, and then Stephen confirmed that our son had been killed in an explosion about ten years ago, that he hadn't felt any pain or had even been aware of what was happening until after it had happened. He made reference to the army, and then confirmed the name of Tony, and specified the year of 1986. He made a joke about the fact that he wasn't getting a message from Elvis, but whoever it was who had passed over had been very obsessed with him, saying that there were hundreds of records and posters... And then came the clincher, because he went on to say that Tony knew that they'd all been sold and that it was the right thing to have done because the money was more important than old memories, and that we should have got rid of it all years before anyway... He also said that if times ever got hard again we could always sell the shirt (this was the one thing we had hung onto) because that would be worth more than all of the other memorabilia put together. He also said that the shirt was in the top draw of the chest of drawers in Tony's old bedroom, wrapped in a plastic bag, along with a photograph of Tony in his dress uniform. These things were all true...'

Jo from Newark: 'I saw Stephen Holbrook at The Palace Theatre in Newark in 1999. He said he wanted to talk to someone who had lost her Mother within the past twelve months, and that this lady would have died as the result of a fall. My Mother had died in 1998 and she had died in exactly those circumstances, so I said yes, and then Stephen started talking about my daughter and about how the way my Mother and I had frequently discussed just how unusual my daughter's eyes are – they're a greeney grey and blue, really very unusual indeed. He gave me the letter J, which is, of course, my own initial, and gave me a date involving the 13th

173

– and my Mum actually died on the 13th. He also said that I'd recently been doing a lot of house alterations and home improvements and that I'd said I wished that Mum was still around to see what I'd done – and he said that she *had* been around and thought that I'd done a lovely job!...'

These are but half a dozen examples from my files and you'll note that it *is* the little things that confirm the links and have so much impact... A St. Christopher medallion, a hand rolled cigarette, a jackdaw, a pair of cowboy boots, Elvis Presley's shirt and an old photograph, a bit of DIY home improvement... These are the things which defy logic and dismiss the concept of there being "plants" in Stephen's audiences. Furthermore, these are the things which make the links so uniquely personal, and in all cases the recipients of the messages have gone away from the demonstrations feeling stronger and more calm and happy than they were before.

As we have said Stephen avoids personal sittings at this stage of his development, and by and large he practices great restraint when it comes to controlling his clairvoyant talents. He tries hard to keep his work "in the right place" i.e. on stage or on the public platform, but even so, there *are* times when he will bring a message through for someone out of this environment. These messages may be short, but they are no less important or evidential for that, and a good case in question is what happened to Gill and Roger Prior.
    In their own words...
    "Sunday 10th February 1991 was a day that would change our lives forever. Our youngest daughter Lisa, just 23, was due home for the half term holiday. She taught at a ballet school in London, and being the fit and very energetic young lady that she was, she had got up early that morning intending to go jogging. But the previous night it had snowed heavily, unusual in London, and the flue to the boiler had become blocked causing fumes to enter the bathroom, which

174

was situated next to the boiler room. Lisa never had a chance and she died within minutes from carbon monoxide poisoning. The first we knew about it was when the phone rang on the Monday morning to say that Lisa had been found dead in her flat.

"We lived the next few days, weeks and months in a never ending nightmare. Surrounded by family and friends offering support and with regular visits from our Minister, we lived on auto-pilot through those terrible days. Our Minister provided a listening ear, but in his own words he said "I do not have all the answers for you." To put our trust in God and believe that Lisa had gone to Heaven just wasn't good enough for us. All her hard work, the heavy exercise regimes, the hours spent at the barre, the trauma of life itself to achieve what one wants – didn't seem to have any point or purpose. Why should we bother if nobody really knew what was at the end of our life down here?

"While we were in this hopeless state of mind someone suggested we visit a Spiritualist Church run by a lady called Una. After a lot of thought and discussion, we decided to take the plunge and go. We knew nothing of what went on at these spooky places, so we did feel a bit nervous and apprehensive. However we needn't have worried! We were amazed by the wonderful atmosphere of love and compassion that exuded from every one we met – although to be honest we were not always impressed by some of the mediums who demonstrated there. In fact, we didn't understand half of what was said.

"Una herself is a lovely person, and as we got to know her better we were touched by her selflessness towards everyone and the time she made for us. It was in this relaxed atmosphere of happiness and love that we were introduced to Stephen who gave regular demonstrations at her church.

"We watched his demonstration one evening and something, somewhere, must have 'clicked' because we both felt drawn towards this young man. The messages he gave to people seemed to be more urgent and more meaningful and comments that probably seemed trivial to others in the congregation seemed to make so much sense to the recipients, and all of the information he gave out seemed to be highly relevant and accurate.

"Chatting to him afterwards he suddenly stopped talking and told Gill that she had recently moved a photograph of Lisa. Gill said "no, definitely not" but Stephen insisted that she had recently done something very significant with our daughter's photograph, and then it suddenly dawned on us that Gill *had* moved a large photo of Lisa from our bedroom into her own room just a few days before; it had been a photograph taken by the ballet school as an advertisement for them and Gill had said that she looked very stern and that she didn't want Lisa looking down on her in that rather haughty way. Stephen also said that one day we would be involved in his kind of work to which we replied "no, not us!""

"We have watched Stephen develop over the years, from being unsure and shy of his mediumship to becoming very sure and trusting in what he is given by his unseen guides. We have spent many an evening talking about how his guides work with him and have become increasingly involved and interested in the philosophy of Spiritualism. We have attended many demonstrations, met hundreds of people and made many new friends, and through all this have watched Stephen grow stronger and more confident over the years. His messages have grown stronger and are always so positive, and the love and compassion he shows to everyone has endeared him to all he meets. He tells people about things he could not possibly know about and he does this time after time. There is only one way in which this is possible – people *must* be communicating with him. It sounds incredible, and so it is, but any rational person must see that this is the only explanation. He is convinced that Lisa is there helping him in the background, which sounds right because she was never very good at pushing herself forwards.

176

"Our friendship has developed from just attending his demonstrations to actually arranging demonstrations for him at new venues, especially now that we have moved down to the South-West... So, this was something else he was right about, because we are now actively involved in his kind of work. Our despair and grief has changed to the knowledge that there must be another life after this one. How else could people communicate with him? How else could he get so much accurate information? He doesn't make any of it up and he couldn't do it just by lucky guesswork.

"We have never actually had a first hand message from Lisa through Stephen; he feels that he knows too much about us to be objective. However this really doesn't matter. It doesn't have the urgency that it once had and we can truly say that meeting Stephen was, and still is, a wonderful and exciting privilege. What he has is so rare and we have never witnessed anything like it. He doesn't know exactly how it all works, only that it does work. It is a gift that has been given to him for a reason and Stephen himself would be the first to say "please don't put me on a pedestal." He is a very unassuming man and a great friend and we take great strength from his words "you cannot die for the life of you!""

If there are any sceptics out there reading this who think these words are just fictional prose, all the parties I have spoken to are more than happy for me to pass on their addresses to any third party so that they may provide independent corroborative evidence. As a matter of common sense, confidentiality and courtesy, I can't publish their personal details in these pages, so may I suggest that any such enquiry be directed through my publishers at Mage Publishing, the address to be found elsewhere at the front piece of this book.

Chapter Twenty One: Who Is Stephen Holbrook?

This is the question that I set out to answer almost one year and eighty thousand words ago. Over the past ten months I have watched scores of his demonstrations, have spent many hours in conversation with him and have conducted dozens of interviews with people who have received some form of message through him from relatives or loved ones who have "died" on this plane of existence. Even so, the answer to what might appear to be such a relatively straight forward question is by no means complete, is by no means clear cut, and no matter how you look at it, is full of contradictions. To quote one of his oldest friends, someone who has been associated with him for almost all of his working life: "You could know Stephen for twenty years and you still wouldn't know all of him."

On stage, when he is demonstrating, he is charged with charismatic energy and the vibrancy of his personality reaches out to touch everyone in the theatre. Off stage and away from the spotlights he is essentially the same. Seldom will you see Stephen Holbrook sitting still and twiddling his thumbs! He is constantly on the go, is always full of enthusiasm and animation, and is always highly articulate. Occasionally he will display a butterfly mind, jumping from one subject to another and leaving his listener lagging behind in a desperate attempt to catch up with the conversation before it shifts onto yet another topic for consideration.

On a purely professional level he takes his work very seriously indeed, and yet quite amazingly (to my way of thinking anyway) he seldom questions his own abilities and has done little to analyse the cause or source of his phenomenal gifts. Once having embraced (or having been embraced by) The Spiritualist Church when he was only sixteen years old, a singular act that put an end to much of his childhood and teenage misery, it seems as though he has taken the presence of a spirit world at its face value, and has got on

178

with the business of living the rest of his life as best he can. This is not to imply that he takes the spirit world for granted – nothing could be further from the truth – but if, for example, I were given the most beautiful motor car in the world, I would want to know what the engine looked like and how it worked. Stephen, on the other hand, is quite content to drive the car without ever looking underneath the bonnet. As a journalist and his biographer I have found this most frustrating at times.

If we are to objectively assess Stephen's work as a clairaudient medium, one must start by doing so subjectively. In my own professional opinion, based on a lifetime dedicated to the subject, I have to say that Stephen is undoubtedly the most powerful medium I have ever come across in twenty years of searching and looking. Eric Hatton, leading light of the Spiritualist National Union, regards Stephen as being "one of the country's top young mediums with tremendous gifts and a formidable talent." Coming from another corner of the field is my old friend Harry Andrews, who like Mr Hatton has also had over forty years' experience in the worlds of clairvoyancy and spiritualism. Harry's view is somewhat more objective inasmuch that for the last thirty odd years he has earned his living by promoting and managing mediums both in this country and in the USA and therefore his view is more in tune with the concept of accuracy rather than the purely *spiritual* content of a medium's message from beyond the veil.

This point needs some elaboration and qualification, and the best way I can do this is to use Harry's own words: "There are too many self styled clairvoyants who talk about spirits and spiritualism and who, when they do bring a message across, waffle on about how much so and so's Mother, or Father, or whoever the link is with, loves them and about how wonderfully at peace they are now that they're with God and good spirits in The Summerlands. These same people usually end up on TV or radio shows talking about "unconditional love" and their first hand visions of Heaven

179

and The Afterlife as shown to them by their various spirit guides: I actually know a number of these guys (and guyesses come to that) who have made hundreds of thousands of dollars writing books just *talking* about mediumship and channelling without actually being able to do it themselves. I totally despise the kind of clairvoyant who goes out there and says *I've got a message from somebody's mother who wants to talk to someone with a bad tummy and this lady is telling me that everything is all right.* Unless they can be more specific than that, although they may not be deliberately conning their audiences, they are still letting their audiences down through want of hard evidence. This is what impresses me so much about Stephen Holbrook. He is precise and specific, and in my opinion he is without doubt the most accurate medium working in Britain today."

I could give you a hundred examples of what Harry is talking about, and a recent demonstration in Lancashire immediately springs to mind.

Stephen is talking to a lady on the front row.

Stephen: 'I'm right in thinking that your partner Chris passed over in November of 1999?'

Lady: 'Yes.'

Stephen: 'And I'm right in thinking that you have got something that belonged to him here with you this evening?'

Lady: 'Yes.'

Stephen: 'You've got his photograph with you!'

Lady: 'Yes.'

Stephen: 'And you've got it in the side pocket of your jeans, attached to something?'

Lady: 'Yes.'

Stephen: 'It's one of those small square laminated photographs that come in a kind of plastic holder, and you've got it attached to his key ring along with his car keys?'

Lady: 'Yes, that's right!'

It is this degree of accuracy that makes Stephen stand out from the crowd. A name, a date, a photograph on a key ring in a jeans pocket!

And yet Stephen takes it all in his stride without any drama or fuss. He does not compare himself to or compete with other mediums – *they do what they do and I do what I do and I suppose we're all trying to do the same thing, aren't we? –* and he fails to recognise that he is something unique and quite special. In fact, if anything, the reverse is true. He is extremely modest and on a personal level, shuns the spotlight and has little or no time for celebrity.

'I'm just me,' he says. 'An ordinary working lad from Wakefield. I'm not an arty farty intellectual and I certainly don't have all the answers to all the questions. I haven't got a philosophy on life, except to say that life is a fantastic gift and we should all do our best to make the very best of it, and I'm *not* at all special. My wife and children are special, my friends and spirit guides are special, and yes, okay, maybe the work that I do is special because it is a bit unusual, isn't it? – But as for me, I'm just the same as anybody else, with just the same worries and concerns... You know, the bills, the mortgage, the kids, the funny banging noise from the back of the car and can we afford a holiday this year or not?'

This is Stephen really "opening up" because normally he keeps his personal thoughts very much to himself. Indeed, despite his charismatic personality he is in essence a very private individual who keeps his personal and professional lives well separated. He is modest in his opinions of himself and to all intents and purposes, he lives a modest lifestyle, smoking the very occasional cigarette, drinking the odd glass of wine, and driving an Austin Montego. He will avoid anything that has got "flash" written on it like the plague, and although he has at times been very enthusiastic about this book project, he has also been extremely concerned that people will think him a bit flash or conceited in lending his

181

name to it. When people like Eric Hatton and Harry Andrews (not to mention the dozens of other people who have contributed their time and testimony to this work) have said kind and positive things about him he has either squirmed with embarrassment or has looked at me with something bordering on incredulity, saying 'did they *really* say that?' or 'oh no, you can't put *that* in the book or people will think I'm too big headed!'

I nod my head wisely, but mentally I wring my hands in despair. It is the nature of his being to be modest and unassuming, and therefore I must accept that he genuinely might not be aware of the tremendous impact he has upon the people he comes into contact with.

He is totally dedicated to his wife and family and it is this degree of dedication that persuades him to do as much as he does to keep them out of the limelight of his public life. He is incredibly generous (sometimes too generous for his own good) both where money matters are concerned (I am aware of that first night up on Ilkley Moor where through want of numbers he waived his usual fee) and perhaps as you might imagine, he is equally generous in spirit, preferring to think the best of someone or something and risk being disappointed rather than thinking the worst, only to have his fears confirmed.

If there is one thing that I have not truly conveyed in this book it is the laughter and the humour, which is such an integral part of this man's life. In all the time I've known him he has never once told me a joke, but in any given demonstration there will always be a few gails of laughter over the course of the evening and on a purely social level, Stephen Holbrook is a fun person to be with and I have taken great and genuine pleasure (as I truly hope I will continue to do) from his company.

But if I am to answer the question: Who is Stephen Holbrook? – and if I am to do it with authority, I must employ a better device than anything used thus far. The onion that I set out to peel in chapter one has been a troublesome vegetable to deal with, for as I have peeled away one layer of the skin I have been confronted with half a dozen more. How then can I sum up my findings to you, the kind soul who has shelled out the better part of seven quid for this strange little book?

There is perhaps a way.

Despite a broad public misconception the lines on the palm of the hand do not give much insight into long journeys across water and nor do they make reference to tall dark handsome strangers. What they *do* give is great insight to a person's character and personality and they *do* draw the reader's attention to areas of strength and weakness within the subject's basic nature. With these thoughts in mind I found myself imagining what I might say to Stephen Holbrook if he turned up at my office for a palm reading. I suspect that it might go a little something like this...

I would start by saying that here was an extremely complicated, contradictory and complex man... A man who was neither shallow nor callow. That here was a man of great sensitivity... I would point out that there were many different definitions of the word "sensitive" and that all of those definitions would be applicable on one level or another. I would put great emphasis on his psychic sensitivity, but I would also home in on his emotional sensitivity too: it isn't going to take much to hurt or upset him – the wrong word at the wrong time from the right person will cut deep and cause hard damage, which is why he will on so many occasions choose to keep his head away from the chopping block of dispute. I would make reference to the way in which he will use his pride as a defence mechanism, and I would elaborate on this by pointing out that this "pride" is not the arrogant kind of pride born of stupidity or ignorance, but the quiet breed of pride born of dignity and an innate sense of right and wrong.

I would describe him as being something of a chameleon with the power to be all things to all people – dining with paupers on Tuesday and Princes on Wednesday and being comfortable and accepted in both echelons of society. I would speak of his willingness to share his laughter and positive energy with all and sundry and then I would take him to task for keeping his tears and anxieties too much to himself. I would acknowledge his honesty and lack of deceit, but I would credit him with his ability to put on a first class act that *does* fool most of the people most of the time.

I would draw his attention to the depth and turbulence of his inner emotions and would probably remark on how difficult it was for him to bring those inner thoughts and feelings to the surface: I would tell him that even when he *could* do this he would frequently choose not to do so, and that although this might provide him with a degree of emotional self preservation, it would frequently create many situations whereby the person that he was and the person other people saw him to be would be two very *different* people.

I would tackle him about his tendency always to put other people and their needs before his own, and how he does this even on occasions when he might be putting his health at risk. I would give him a very hard time for succumbing to the Taurean trait of being his own worse critic... Illuminating out of all proportion what he considered to be his shortcomings and failures without giving himself due credit for the things that he did well and got right... And, if I were being really vicious, I would make some remark about a fundamental lack of self confidence and self esteem that frequently hid behind that veil of modesty.

Credit would be paid to his deep sense of loyalty, commitment and responsibility, but it would be pointed out that far too frequently others benefited far more from these qualities than he did himself. The "loyalty" aspect would be explored further and it would be pointed out that along with the obvious loyalties towards family and blood ties (which would be incredibly strong) there would also be an ardent quality of loyalty towards friends. That this "loyalty" trait could be taken to extremes – loyalty to the corner shop, to a particular brand product, even to an old car that was long past its prime.

Stephen would be described as a "giver" rather than a "taker" but one, who in the very act of giving, knew that he might never get anything in return – but who would give all he had to give anyway.

His natural caution would be highlighted, along with his wariness of change: his need to test the water with his elbow before he jumped in with both feet!

I would tease him about his honesty and tell him that I would never doubt what he told me, but that I might seriously worry about some of the things he might choose *not* to tell me. I would appreciate that this would not be done through deceit, but through compassion, for if by *not* telling me about something that I might worry about, I couldn't worry about it, could I? – And therefore he would be doing me a service and a kindness.

I would make some mention of his temper – how it is very well controlled, but how never-the-less it still exists. This temper will be born of frustration and injustice, and there may be no more than half a dozen times in the whole of his life when he actually loses it – but when he *does* lose it, watch out because the fallout will be monumental. Reference would be made to his ability to forgive, but a basic *inability* to forget. He won't carry grudges but he has got a long memory!

Finally, because it is such an essential part of his life, I would make reference to his spirituality, and I would want to talk about that at some length because he doesn't come over as a particularly spiritual person – certainly not in the ethereal holier than thou sense, anyway. On the contrary, there is a lovely earthy straight dealing feet on the ground energy that is as endearing as it is appealing and makes one think of mischievous school boys and out of work actors in search of adventure.

And yet I would want to reassure him that the spirituality *is* there, and be it latent or blatant, it is there like a rock providing a spiritual pathway leading into an unknown future in which it is inevitable that he should reach out, touch souls, remove some of the fear of death and bring just a little glimmer of light into the darkness of our lives.

And for this, Stephen Holbrook, on behalf of us all, I thank you very much indeed!

Last Word – Stephen on Stephen

I'm not a patient person – in fact I'm very impatient. If things don't happen straight away I can get very uptight. Even as a kid, my Mum used to call me 90mph Joe – I was never still – always had to be doing something, never satisfied – nothing was ever enough. My wife says I'm still like that... Asking what's for tea when we're still only half way through lunch! Despite the way I come over on stage, I'm very underconfident. I question everything and I have a great problem accepting any kind of praise. My biggest hang-up is trying to please everyone all at the same time. There is nothing very exciting about me. I'm not an exciting person. Apart from this unusual gift that I've got, I'm just a bloody hairdresser....